THE
OTHER
HALF
OF THE
ARMY

THE OTHER HALF OF THE ARMY

Women in Kingdom Ministry

•PHILL OLSON•

The Other Half of the Army; Women in Kingdom Ministry by Phill Olson

© Copyright 2017 - Phill Olson, Mechanicsburg, PA. All rights reserved.

ISBN. 978-1-944238-09-4

Apostolic Network of Global Awakening
1451 Clark Street
Mechanicsburg, PA 17055
globalawakeningstore.com

For more information on how to order this book or any of the other materials that Global Awakening offers, please contact the Global Awakening Store.

Scriptures marked NIV are taken from the NEW INTERNATIONAL VERSION (NIV): Scripture taken from the Holy Bible, NEW INTERNATIONAL VERSION®. Copyright© 1973, 1978, 1984, 2011 by Biblica, Inc.™ Used by permission of Zondervan.

Scriptures marked NASB are taken from the NEW AMERICAN STANDARD (NAS): Scripture taken from the NEW AMERICAN STANDARD BIBLE®, Copyright© 1960, 1962, 1963,1968, 1971, 1972, 1973, 1975, 1977, 1995 by The Lockman Foundation. Used by permission.

Scriptures marked ESV are taken from the Holy Bible, ENGLISH STANDARD VERSION (ESV): Scriptures taken from the Holy Bible, ENGLISH STANDARD VERSION ®, Copyright© 2001 by Crossway, a publishing ministry of Good News Publishers. Used by permission.

Scriptures marked NLT are taken from the Holy Bible, New Living Translation, Copyright©1996, 2004, 2007, 2013 by Tyndale House Foundation. Used by permission of Tyndale House Publishers, Inc., Carol Stream, Illinois 60188. All rights reserved.

Scriptures marked THE MESSAGE. Copyright© by Eugene H. Peterson 1993, 1994, 1995, 1996, 2000, 2001, 2002. Used by permission of Tyndale House Publishers, Inc.

Cover illustration & interior page design by Daniel St. Armand

Table of Contents

ENDORSEMENTS	i
ACKNOWLEDGEMENTS	iii
FORWARD	v
PREFACE	vii
FIRST CHAPTER	1
SECOND CHAPTER	7
THIRD CHAPTER	11
FOURTH CHAPTER	27
FIFTH CHAPTER	39
SIXTH CHAPTER	69
SEVENTH CHAPTER	75
EPILOGUE	97
PARTIAL BIBLIOGRAPHY	103

Endorsements

Phill Olson has done a fine job of showing from Scripture that in the New Covenant women stand equally with men and have an equal right to be ministers of the Gospel. Our Father is in the process of helping us get rid of traditional teachings that cripple "half of the army," and allowing them the place that He intended for them.

Joe McIntyre
Senior Minister at Word of His Grace Church and author at Empowering Grace Ministries

"Phill Olson has demonstrated personally and professionally a passion to correct centuries of poor hermeneutics and even worse application in the church in the controversy surrounding the gift of women to the church. As a pastor, school director and teacher, he brings fresh revelation that releases all women into their destiny as disciples, leaders and culture shapers. I highly recommend this teaching resource."

Dr. Mike Hutchings,
Director,
Global School of Supernatural Ministry and
Global Certification Programs
Global Awakening

Well, this is definitely my new favorite resource on the topic of women in leadership. Phill Olson gets right to the point and follows the topic straight through the Bible, from the beginning to the end, and smooths out the "bumps" along the way. In under 110 pages, many people will be transformed and set free with this truth.

Dr. Jonathan Welton
Best-selling author and President of Welton Academy

I find this book simple, direct and powerful in deconstructing false perspectives on women in ministry while simultaneously opening up the gate further with an invitation to go in. Phill has a unique way of laying down the facts – hard earned bricks of truth that feel somehow more like feathers to the reader. I appreciate the searching out of the scriptures while keeping the reader moving with a natural narrative style. I express my whole-hearted support for this to be distributed far and wide and I thank Phill for fighting for me – for us – for women who are called of God to lead.

Katie Luse
On-site Administrator
Global School of Supernatural Ministry
Mechanicsburg, PA

Acknowledgements

I note in the first section of this booklet, that my views on the topic of women in ministry have shifted over time and with good reason. I have had some people touch my life in powerful ways, which caused me to rethink my position. So I thank my younger daughter, Cheryl, for challenging me to read Lee Grady's book, 10 Lies the Church Tells Women, which began my process of digging more deeply in Scripture to see if his conclusions about including women in leadership capacities in the church were accurate.

While attending Randy Clark's Global School of Supernatural Ministry in 2007, we had the pleasure of having Lee teach with us for a week. He prophesied over my wife and me that we would be used by the Lord to bring freedom to women for ministry. He saw a picture of me with a large pair of wire cutters, which I would be using to free women from the cages that have held them captive.

Our pastor Dave Hess preached a sermon series on women and ministry, and listening to his thoughts and interpretation of the biblical texts helped push me further into study. When called to lead a ministry training school in South Africa in 2010, I realized that if I were to teach men and women how to respond to God's direction for their lives, I should clarify my thinking about women in church leadership in particular.

My wife, Barbara clearly demonstrates that women can readily respond to God's call to teach, preach and lead in the family of God with great effectiveness. To all these influencers, my heartfelt thanks.

Finally, I am extremely grateful to my editor Amanda Vigneaud. Your enthusiasm for the book and strategic guidance has enabled me to revisit the text and stay focused on the main themes. Your input has been invaluable in making this work stronger.

I am also extremely grateful for the patience of the Holy Spirit as my teacher while wading through many contributions of people offering a broad spectrum of views on this subject. I sense very strongly that we live in a time when God is calling His church to get outside its four walls and actively co-labor with Him to bring more of heaven to earth. He wants as many active participants as possible, so it is time for the whole church to recognize His call to the other half of the army.

Foreword

From Randy Clark

Phill Olson's The Other Half of the Army is a masterpiece. Dealing with the subject of women in leadership, it is powerful for its faithfulness to consider the fullness of the biblical position on this subject. Years ago, a short book on the Kingdom of God, by George Eldon Ladd became a game changer for understanding the Kingdom. I believe The Other Half of the Army will be a game changer in regard to the issue of women and ministry, as well as leadership. First and foremost, Phill wanted to handle the total teaching of Scripture fairly and faithfully. I have known Phill for many years, and I can attest to his honor of Scripture and wanting to be faithful to Scripture.

I really appreciated his dealing with the difficult texts of Scripture, not ignoring them, but handling them fairly. Failure to have done this would have been a weaker book. I agree with Phill's final conclusion.

I appreciated the section that revealed the effects of church tradition upon biblical interpretation as well. For me, failure to see the impact of church tradition upon historical theology makes a book weaker. Though this is a short book it is not a weak book. Phill gets quickly to the point and makes his point.

This book should be read by women who wonder if it is God's will for them to be in ministry; by men who wonder if it is okay for women to be in ministry; and by men who believe women have no place in ministry. Phill's argument derived from Scripture could help those male leaders unleash half of God's army. I highly recommend this book to you. Thank you Phill for this labor of love on your part for all those who are in Christ.

Dr. Randy Clark
Overseer of the Apostolic Network of Global Awakening;
Author of Baptized in the Spirit, The Authority to Heal, The Healing Breakthrough, and There Is More!

Preface

When I finished this book in its initial draft, I felt satisfied that the project was finally finished. But as I left the manuscript on my computer, I wondered whether I should take more time with it before pursuing its publication. During that interval, I received a prophetic word from a trusted brother who said, "You have a book in your computer that needs to be published, so what are you waiting for?" Following that interaction, I had the idea that the book would have more life if I included some real stories of women in ministry and the challenges they have faced along the way in their journey of serving the Lord.

In the early months of our return to the US, I interviewed four women to give the reader some additional understanding as to why I embarked upon this project. Though I exercised some editorial freedom by changing some names and places, the stories themselves are real.

I want to thank each of these wonderful ladies for taking the time to share their stories and for being transparent about what they have faced in the past and, at times, still do. Each of them is a faithful follower of Jesus who is making a positive impact in the lives of people by revealing the Kingdom of God. Their ministries reflect the love of our Savior Jesus, and I am grateful they have answered His call with courage and determination. I know my life is better having experienced their influence.

First Chapter

WHY THIS BOOK?

Ten years ago, had someone suggested that I write a book on the role of women in church and ministry, I would have quickly declined; I struggled inwardly with what I had been taught versus what I wanted to believe. From my training in the church, I learned women should not be allowed to take on leadership roles because they lacked the authority to do so. However, my experience working with women in ministry clearly contradicted that view; I regularly saw women exercising spiritual gifts and speaking into other people's lives with great authority. There was a conflict in my thinking begging for resolution that I temporarily chose to ignore. In the past decade, however, I have undergone significant life changes that have shifted some of my previously held beliefs regarding women in the church. Before we come to those changes, let me first offer a very brief overview of my experiences leading up to that period in my life.

After committing my life to Jesus in the summer of 1971, I slowly moved away from my pursuit of medicine and instead chose to attend seminary. Following graduation, my wife and I moved to Ohio where I began 10 years of pastoral ministry. In 1987, I left full-time ministry and began a career in the business world which continued for 20 years. In 2003, things began to shift. First, my wife, Barb, and I led a short-term missions team from our church to share the Gospel at a youth camp in the Zelenogorsk region in Russia. It was my first time traveling abroad and our first short-term mission trip, so we felt more dependent on God than ever before. Stepping into a foreign culture with very little understanding of the language left us entirely reliant on native interpreters and brought us to a new place of humility. God was working to help us understand our call.

Another shift in our lives came in 2006, as we both made a decision to leave our respective careers to attend a ministry training school under the leadership of Randy Clark. We desired to know God's plan for us to "finish well." During our time at the Global School of Supernatural Ministry, we were continually challenged to refresh our understanding to live and walk by the Spirit. After those life-changing years, we responded to a very direct call from God and moved from Pennsylvania to South Africa. From 2010 to 2015, we served as directors of the team running a ministry school similar to the one we attended in the States.

Our move to South Africa came at a critical time. I was thinking a great deal about current views of women in church leadership. At the Global School of Supernatural Ministry – South Africa, a number of our students were women fervently pursuing God's Kingdom. Among these, many felt God was calling them to leadership. Our school's staff, comprised of Americans and South Africans, understood the importance of encouraging these women to pursue their God-given destinies. We also knew, based on our history in various church settings, that they could face some opposition should they pursue leadership in the church. I believe that such resistance is, at least partially, rooted in hundreds of years of church tradition. I believe it also has its basis in a misunderstanding of certain passages of Scripture that at first glance seem to support a male-centered hierarchy of church leadership. I have read many excellent books on this topic, both from *egalitarian* and *complementarian* views, and I have wrestled with the Scriptures throughout this process. In this book, I hope to explain that the biblical perspective supports a view of men and women ministering together with equal status, working to bring the world into alignment with the heavenly Kingdom. As someone who firmly believes in the authority and integrity of the Bible, my goal is to share clearly how and why I have reached my present position. Since we have been given the responsibility of co-laboring with God to bring heaven to earth, we need the whole army engaged.

I want to be clear from the outset that this has been a long journey for me. When I first came to know the Lord, I was part of a small charismatic fellowship at the college I attended. All of us were very young believers and had not yet been exposed to much church tradition. The whole fellowship, men and women, felt free to exercise the gifts of the Holy Spirit as we met and worshipped. But even in that setting, all of the male leaders held the opinion that women should not be pastors and that all women, in general, should submit to all men. When I went to seminary, I witnessed more of the influence of traditional interpretations of Scripture. I often heard from those around me that women should not pursue ordination to become pastors or elders/leaders in the local church, but should serve only as Christian education directors or leaders of women's ministries. That opinion is based on several New Testament passages, which we will examine later in this study. Because I held our teachers in high regard, I tried to fit my experience with women exercising spiritual gifts into that understanding, however it always left me discomfited.

When I think back to my ordination council in 1977, I remember a group of people gathered in a church in northeastern Massachusetts for the purpose of determining what I believed and if I should be recommended for ordination. At that point in my life, I felt very strongly that women should freely move in the gifts of the Spirit (they should pray, prophesy, lay hands on the sick, etc.), but they should not be recognized as lead pastors or church elders. I wrestled with that view because there were times when it felt like I was trying to push a square peg into a round hole; something did not fit. The dividing line seemed a bit artificial to me. I wondered why we believed it was acceptable to send women into the mission field as the sole spiritual leader for an unreached people group, but when they returned home we permitted them only to "share" and not to preach. Relegating such "sharing" to church suppers and ladies' teas represented a real disconnect in thinking.

When I defended my position during my ordination, it was obvious the audience was puzzled by my beliefs. At that point, I was still wrestling with passages in Scripture that I believed clearly taught women should not be in positions of leadership. I maintained that tenuous position for a long time. About 15 years later, I revisited those passages to see if I had interpreted them correctly. At that time, I read Lee Grady's book *10 Lies the Church Tells Women*. After some conversations with my younger daughter, who was also grappling with this issue, I decided to look more closely at the passages in question. I read about Deborah and Huldah, Miriam and Priscilla, Phoebe and Junia. I also heard stories about great women leaders, past and present, like Aimee Semple-McPherson, Maria Woodworth-Etter, Heidi Baker and Michelle Perry. It was very clear that God has used and is using women as leaders in powerful ways to advance His Kingdom. So, like a good Berean, I felt compelled to revisit this potentially thorny issue. In my search, I found that Scripture clearly emphasizes that God's design is for battles to be waged by men and women, side by side.

THE OTHER HALF OF THE ARMY

Second Chapter

AN EMPHASIS FROM THE BEGINNING OF HUMAN HISTORY

For us to do this study justice, we need to go back to the beginning of Scripture to understand God's view of men and women. The question in my mind is whether we have placed constraints and limitations on women in general, and in leadership in particular, based on a very small number of verses which do not match the overall emphasis of Scripture. Is it possible, due to long-standing cultural traditions both within the church and without, that we have misinterpreted some of Paul's writings, thereby refusing the influence of women? I think so. I also think that the perspective and intuition of women could assist us as we face our daily spiritual battles as individuals and as a church body.

Let us begin by looking at Genesis chapter one, verses 26 and 27.

> *Then God said, "Let us make human beings in our image, to be like us. They will reign over the fish in the sea, the birds in the sky, the livestock, all the wild animals on the earth, and the small ani-*

mals that scurry along the ground." So God created human beings in his own image. In the image of God he created them; male and female he created them. (Genesis 1:26-27, NLT)

Every woman and every man contain the imago dei, the image of God. I purposely chose the New Living Translation for this passage because it correctly translates the Hebrew word "Adam" as "human beings" instead of "man."[1] The context here demands an inclusive understanding: men and women. We can conclude from these early creation passages that there are both female and male characteristics in the Godhead: Father, Son and Holy Spirit (note the plural us in verse 26). For example, in Scripture God is compared to a father.

> The Lord is like a father to his children, tender and compassionate to those who fear him. (Psalm 103:13)

There are 112 references to God as father in John's Gospel alone. We also see that God is compared to a mother in multiple passages:

> Yet Jerusalem says, "The Lord has deserted us; the Lord has forgotten us." Never! Can a mother forget her nursing child? Can she feel no love for the child she has borne? But even if that were possible, I would not forget you! See, I have written your name on the palms of my hands. (Isaiah 49:14-16)

> I will comfort you there in Jerusalem as a mother comforts her child. (Isaiah 66:13)

> O Jerusalem, Jerusalem, the city that kills the prophets and stones God's messengers! How often I have wanted to gather your children together as a hen protects her chicks beneath her wings, but you wouldn't let me. (Luke 13:34, NLT)

---

1 (ā ḏām): n.masc.; person, human, i.e., a single human being of either sex (Ps 49:21), humankind, mankind, a class of being created by God without regard to sex, with a focus as a class of creature. James A. Swanson. Dictionary of Biblical Languages with Semantic Domains: Hebrew (Old Testament). (Oak Harbor: Logos Research Systems, Inc., 1997)

It is important for us to keep in mind that, even though we may imagine God to have primarily male characteristics, Scripture demonstrates both male and female characteristics are inherent in his nature.

Additional passages from Genesis show that God created men and women with equal status. In Genesis 1:26, God says that "they" will reign over the creation. Since God uses the term for human beings, he intends for men and women to exercise dominion together. Genesis 2:18 in the New Living Translation says, "Then the Lord God said, 'It is not good for the man to be alone. I will make a helper who is just right for him.'" The New American Standard Bible translates it slightly differently (and here I am using the margin note), "Then the Lord God said, 'It is not good for the man to be alone; I will make him a helper corresponding to him.'" In Hebrew, the words "helper" and "corresponding to" are *ezer kenegdo*. *Ezer* is traditionally translated "helper,"[2] but should not be read as inferior or subservient. In 16 of its 19 uses in the Old Testament, this word is used with regard to God's help in might or power. For example, in Psalm 70:5:

> *But I am poor and needy; hasten to me, O God! You are my help and my deliverer; O LORD, do not delay! (ESV)*

Or, consider Psalm 121:1-2:

> *I lift up my eyes to the hills. From where does my help come? My help comes from the LORD, who made heaven and earth. (ESV)*

In both of these instances, "help" refers to God's help. The He-

---

2 עֵזֶר *(ezer) 1. help, support (Is. 30:5) 2. a helper (Gen 2:18, 20). William Lee Holladay.. A concise Hebrew and Aramaic lexicon of the Old Testament. (Leiden: Brill, 2000)*

brew word *kenegdo* has a meaning "of equal standing."[3] In Eve, God provided a partner who could mirror Adam's skills and abilities in an equal and complementary fashion. This was the established male/female relationship until the events of Genesis 3. As I mentioned earlier, we must keep in mind those early verses in Genesis,

> *Then God said, "Let us make mankind in our image, in our likeness, so that they may rule over the fish in the sea and the birds in the sky, over the livestock and all the wild animals, and over all the creatures that move along the ground."...God blessed them and said to them, "Be fruitful and increase in number; fill the earth and subdue it. Rule over the fish in the sea and the birds in the sky and over every living creature that moves on the ground." Genesis 1:26, 28 (NIV).*

There is no sense of superiority in either partner; instead, both man and woman are called to rule and reign in mutual effort and to fill the earth with the glory of God.

---

3 נֶגְדּוֹ. *(negda) orig. noun, opposite, counterpart, only in kenegdô like his counterpart = corresponding to him Genesis 2:18, 20. William Lee Holladay.. A concise Hebrew and Aramaic lexicon of the Old Testament. (Leiden: Brill, 2000)*

Third Chapter

THE ROOT OF THE PROBLEM

Despite God's clear warning in Scripture for Adam and Eve not to eat from the tree of knowledge, it was not long before the first couple made a choice to disobey Him. Eating of the tree of knowledge changed everything, as God said it would, and Satan knew that. Before considering the consequences of Adam and Eve's actions, let us examine in greater detail what took place in the garden that fateful day.

There has been a tendency among some church leaders to place the blame for all the sin in the world on Eve's action: eating the forbidden fruit. After all, Adam was clearly directed by God not to eat of the fruit of that particular tree, and yet Eve did. However, it is important to note in Genesis 3:6 that "Then she gave some [of the fruit] to her husband, who was with her."... Note that every occurrence of the word "you" in chapter 3 verses 1-5 is in the plural. Before Eve was created, Adam had been charged to tend and guard the garden (Gen. 2:15), a role he was supposed to fulfill even after she was by his side. Not only had the serpent gained access to the garden, Adam made no effort to stop Eve from disobeying God's command. He not only watched her disobey, he also shared in eating the fruit when she offered it to him. It is very clear from the passage that we cannot place sole responsibility on Eve's shoulders for the entrance of sin into the world. We need only read from 1 Corinthians 15 to gain a proper perspective.

> *For since death came through a man, the resurrection of the dead comes also through a man. For as in Adam all die, so in Christ all will be made alive. (1 Corinthians 15: 21-22, NIV)*

When God visited with Adam and Eve later that day we begin to see the consequences of their disobedience. First, they hid from the Lord, which reveals their fractured intimacy with Him. Next, they tried to shift blame: Adam accused Eve, Eve blamed the serpent. It quickly becomes clear, the couple's gained "knowledge" only brought them to a place of isolation and fear.

Later, in Genesis 3:14-15, we read:

> *So the LORD God said to the serpent, "Because you have done this, cursed are you above all livestock and all wild animals! You will crawl on your belly and you will eat dust all the days of your life. And I will put enmity between you and the woman, and between your offspring and hers; he will crush your head, and you will strike his heel." (NIV)*

From this time on, there is enmity, or extreme hatred, between Satan and the woman because he knows from this prophetic word in verse 15 that a woman will ultimately bring into the world the one who will ensure his destruction. Because women represent the Christ-bearing one, they are the targets of intense spiritual warfare as the enemy tries to marginalize and minimize their influence in virtually every culture in the world. We will examine more evidence of this as we continue in our study.

Further effects of the original act of disobedience are seen in the next verse, Genesis 3:16, but are rendered differently depending on the translation:

> *To the woman he said, "I will make your pains in childbearing very severe; with painful labor you will give birth to children. Your desire will be for your husband, and he will rule over you." (NIV)*

> *To the woman He said, "I will greatly multiply your pain in childbirth, in pain you will bring forth children; yet your desire will be for your husband, and he will rule over you." (NASB)*

> *Then he said to the woman, "I will sharpen the pain of your pregnancy, and in pain you will give birth. And you will desire to control your husband, but he will rule over you." (NLT)*

I have given three examples of translation here to show how translators can influence our understanding of the text. Both the NIV and NASB say that the woman's desire shall be for her husband. In my opinion, this translation does not reflect the intention of the Hebrew text. The New Living Translation gives a better rendering of the Hebrew verb, *teshukatek*, which reflects a desire to control (such as in Genesis 4:7, where Cain is warned of the controlling influence of sin).[1] The verse shows there will be an ongoing battle for control and superiority between the sexes. That struggle continues to haunt us many millennia later. The curse resulting from that initial act of disobedience has woven its influence throughout succeeding generations of humanity. In spite of that consequence, however, we know that under the New Covenant, Jesus redeemed us from that curse (Galatians 3:13). That is why there is hope for men and women, wives and husbands, not only to live peacefully with each other, but also to stand together in unity to bring heaven to earth. That was, in part, Jesus' purpose when He prayed the high priestly prayer in John 17, particularly the following verses:

> *My prayer is not for them alone. I pray also for those who will believe in me through their message, that all of them may be one, Father, just as you are in me and I am in you. May they also be in us so that the world may believe that you have sent me. I have given them the glory that you gave me, that they may be one as we are one—I in them and you in me—so that they may be brought to complete unity. Then the world will know that you sent me and have loved them even as you have loved me. (John 17: 20-23, NIV)*

Because Jesus was speaking, I know that God continues to honor this prayer. I believe that we are seeing greater unity growing among all believers as the full Gospel of the Kingdom is shared in word and power. We see barriers being removed related to race, economic status and, particularly, gender in these days as we seek to co-labor with God, as a full army, to bring His Kingdom to earth.

---

1 הָקְוּשָׁת *(tešû·qā(h))(teshukah): n.fem.;* ≡ *Str 8669; TWOT 2352a—LN 25.12–25.32 desire, urges, longing, i.e., a very strong emotion or feeling to have or do something (Ge 3:16; 4:7; SS 7:11[EB 10]+), note: this strong desire may refer to sexual urges or desires, or a desire to dominate, or just be independent of the man, other references may also be possible.*

FEMALE LEADERS IN THE OLD TESTAMENT

Before we shift to consider the New Covenant understanding of women, we must highlight some female leaders we find in the Old Testament. Even under the older covenant, which appears at first glance to be heavily male dominated, there are demonstrations of God's original intent for men and women to share the responsibilities of leadership. For example, there are two references to Miriam being a prophet and leader.

> *Then Miriam the prophet, Aaron's sister, took a timbrel in her hand, and all the women followed her, with timbrels and dancing. (Exodus 15: 20, NIV)*

This passage speaks of Miriam as a prophet who led the victory song after the Egyptians had been drowned in the Red Sea. Later in Micah, we find her listed with Moses and Aaron as those who led Israel out of Egypt.

> *I brought you up out of Egypt and redeemed you from the land of slavery, sent Moses to lead you, also Aaron and Miriam. (Micah 6:4, NIV)*

Huldah is listed as a prophet in 2 Kings.

> *Hilkiah the priest, Ahikam, Akbor, Shaphan and Asaiah went to speak to the prophet Huldah, who was the wife of Shallum son of Tikvah, the son of Harhas, keeper of the wardrobe. She lived in Jerusalem, in the New Quarter. (2 Kings 22:14, NIV)*

In verses 15 through 20, we see that Huldah was so highly respected, a contingent of male leaders sought a prophetic word of guidance from her in a time of crisis to bring back to King Josiah.

There is also mention that Isaiah's wife was recognized as a prophet in Isaiah 8.

> *Then I made love to the prophetess, and she conceived and gave birth to a son. And the Lord said to me, "Name him Maher-Shalal-Hash-Baz." (Isaiah 8:3, NIV)*

Deborah receives a bit more attention than other women and is highlighted in Judges chapters 4 and 5. Deborah was not only a prophet and a judge, but also served as a military leader who brought Israel out from the oppressive rule of Jabin. We see clearly the honor she was shown in Judges 4.

> *Now Deborah, a prophet, the wife of Lappidoth, was leading Israel at that time. She held court under the Palm of Deborah between Ramah and Bethel in the hill country of Ephraim, and the Israelites went up to her to have their disputes decided. (Judges 4:4-5, NIV)*

When Deborah suggested Barak lead an army against Sisera, Jabin's general, Barak refused the notion until she agreed to accompany his troops. Ultimately another woman, Jael, was honored for the victory of killing Sisera while he slept in her camp.

Though we do not have many examples, there were women who held respected positions of leadership in the Old Testament. It is notable that even under the primarily male hierarchical old covenant, women led militarily, spoke prophetically and gave respected spiritual input. While the shift to include women is more obvious under the New Covenant, even under the more patriarchal views of Old Testament thinking, we can see the full participation of women in God's army is a constant theme in the heart of God.

THE ROLE OF WOMEN IN THE INTER-TESTAMENTAL PERIOD

During the 400-year period between the writings of the Old and New Testaments, often called the period of silence, Greek philosophy and culture gained influence throughout the civilized world. The subjugation of women spread and traditional Jewish family values were overshadowed, negatively influencing attitudes towards females in society. During this period, women faced increasing constraints in society, particularly regarding public behavior. Jewish women were not allowed to speak in the synagogue and were restricted to the outer courts. They were not allowed to study the Scriptures, nor were they permitted to read Scripture aloud publicly. When out of their homes, they could not speak with men apart from their husbands. The Pandora myth, which attributed all cultural and relational problems to women, generally became more accepted as truth. Women were also not allowed to testify in court, as they were considered "unreliable witnesses." The Hellenization of first century culture devalued women to a place that ranked them barely above slaves, mere chattel for the nurture of babies and food preparation for the family. The ever-burgeoning effects of the curse unfolded as men oppressed women through attitudes of superiority in word and deed.[2]

JESUS' HEART FOR WOMEN

If we have any doubts about the heart of God toward women, we need only look to Jesus. In a culture steeped in male superiority and domination of women, our amazing Redeemer modeled a radically different perspective and worldview. The Savior was born into the world by the obedience of a woman. Mary's interaction with Gabriel in Luke 1 is an outstanding example of

---

2 Elizabeth Tetlow. *Women and Ministry in the New Testament*. (Paulist Press, 1980).

simple obedience to a prophetic word from the Lord. When the angel Gabriel says to her in Luke 1:37, "No spoken word of God is impossible," her response was submission, which was no small decision given her state. Pledged in marriage, Mary risked not only rejection by her fiancé, but also conviction of adultery, punishable by death, from religious leaders in her community. At a minimum, she risked the life-long stigma of bearing a child out of wedlock and ostracization by other women in her village. Mary's trust in God was immense, and, through her faith, God's plan to save humanity was fulfilled.

Throughout Scripture, Jesus treated women with matchless love and respect, as seen in the story of the woman at the well in John 4.

> *Now he had to go through Samaria. So he came to a town in Samaria called Sychar, near the plot of ground Jacob had given to his son Joseph. Jacob's well was there, and Jesus, tired as he was from the journey, sat down by the well. It was about noon. When a Samaritan woman came to draw water, Jesus said to her, "Will you give me a drink?" (His disciples had gone into the town to buy food.) The Samaritan woman said to him, "You are a Jew and I am a Samaritan woman. How can you ask me for a drink?" (For Jews do not associate with Samaritans.)*

> *Jesus answered her, "If you knew the gift of God and who it is that asks you for a drink, you would have asked him and he would have given you living water." "Sir," the woman said, "you have nothing to draw with and the well is deep. Where can you get this living water? Are you greater than our father Jacob, who gave us the well and drank from it himself, as did also his sons and his livestock?" Jesus answered, "Everyone who drinks this water will be thirsty again, but whoever drinks the water I give them will never thirst. Indeed, the water I give them will become in them a spring of water welling up to eternal life."*

The woman said to him, "Sir, give me this water so that I won't get thirsty and have to keep coming here to draw water." He told her, "Go, call your husband and come back." "I have no husband," she replied. Jesus said to her, "You are right when you say you have no husband. The fact is, you have had five husbands, and the man you now have is not your husband. What you have just said is quite true." "Sir," the woman said, "I can see that you are a prophet. Our ancestors worshiped on this mountain, but you Jews claim that the place where we must worship is in Jerusalem." "Woman," Jesus replied, "believe me, a time is coming when you will worship the Father neither on this mountain nor in Jerusalem. You Samaritans worship what you do not know; we worship what we do know, for salvation is from the Jews. Yet a time is coming and has now come when the true worshipers will worship the Father in the Spirit and in truth, for they are the kind of worshipers the Father seeks. God is spirit, and his worshipers must worship in the Spirit and in truth." The woman said, "I know that Messiah" (called Christ) "is coming. When he comes, he will explain everything to us." Then Jesus declared, "I, the one speaking to you—I am he."

...Many of the Samaritans from that town believed in him because of the woman's testimony, "He told me everything I ever did." So when the Samaritans came to him, they urged him to stay with them, and he stayed two days. And because of his words many more became believers. They said to the woman, "We no longer believe just because of what you said; now we have heard for ourselves, and we know that this man really is the Savior of the world." (John 4:2-26; 39-42, NIV)

Several observations can be made regarding this passage. First, Jesus approached the woman in public, rather than ignoring or avoiding her, as was the custom at the time. Second, Jesus addressed her, in spite of the fact that she was a Samaritan, an act considered off limits by practicing Jews at the time due to the Samaritans' violation of the Law and their rejection of Jerusalem as the center of worship. Third, Jesus attended to her despite her sinful lifestyle, a five-time divorcee living with a man outside of marriage. Despite the apparent barriers, nothing kept Jesus from initiating a life-changing conversation with the woman at the well. The encounter impacted her so deeply, she became an early evangelist, taking her story back to the community so that others might turn to the Savior. By refusing to uphold the cultural expectations of his time, Jesus was able to reject a religious patriarchal spirit and release the woman at the well into her calling. Had Jesus not overcome these socio-cultural barriers, the entire community would have failed to benefit from one woman's evangelistic invitation to encounter salvation.

From John, we see that Jesus was definitely exerting a counter-cultural influence in his treatment of women. Consider this quote from Jeremias' *Jerusalem in the Time of Jesus*. "Eastern women take no part in public life. This was true in the time of Jesus, in all cases where Jewish families faithfully observed the Law. When the Jewess of Jerusalem left her house, her face was hidden by an arrangement of two head veils, a head-band on the forehead with bands to the chin, and a hairnet with ribbons and knots so that her features could not be recognized."[3] We see Jesus moving against this patriarchal spirit in Luke 7.

> *When one of the Pharisees invited Jesus to have dinner with him, he went to the Pharisee's house and reclined at the table. A woman in that town who lived a sinful life learned that Jesus was eating at the Pharisee's house, so she came there with an alabaster jar of perfume. As she stood behind him at his feet weeping, she began*

---

[3] Joachim Jeremias. *Jerusalem in the Time of Jesus*. (Philadelphia, PA : Fortress Press, 1969).

to wet his feet with her tears. Then she wiped them with her hair, kissed them and poured perfume on them. When the Pharisee who had invited him saw this, he said to himself, "If this man were a prophet, he would know who is touching him and what kind of woman she is—that she is a sinner." Jesus answered him, "Simon, I have something to tell you." "Tell me, teacher," he said. "Two people owed money to a certain moneylender. One owed him five hundred denarii, and the other fifty. Neither of them had the money to pay him back, so he forgave the debts of both. Now which of them will love him more?" Simon replied, "I suppose the one who had the bigger debt forgiven." "You have judged correctly," Jesus said.

Then he turned toward the woman and said to Simon, "Do you see this woman? I came into your house. You did not give me any water for my feet, but she wet my feet with her tears and wiped them with her hair. You did not give me a kiss, but this woman, from the time I entered, has not stopped kissing my feet. You did not put oil on my head, but she has poured perfume on my feet. Therefore, I tell you, her many sins have been forgiven—as her great love has shown. But whoever has been forgiven little loves little."

Then Jesus said to her, "Your sins are forgiven." The other guests began to say among themselves, "Who is this who even forgives sins?" Jesus said to the woman, "Your faith has saved you; go in peace." (Luke 7:36-50, NIV)

In this story, Jesus visited with a Pharisee named Simon. It was probably a high point in this man's life to host Jesus and share a meal with him. I am quite certain, however, that Simon had no grid for what would unfold as the evening progressed. An unnamed woman of questionable reputation crashed his party and placed herself at Jesus' feet, weeping and anointing him with expensive perfume. As the text tells us, Simon was quite indignant, assuming if Jesus were truly a prophet, he would have known about this woman. And why did she think she could invade a party of men in the first place? He should never have let her come near him, rendering him unclean. But Jesus, after confronting Simon with his pointed question, declared her forgiven and blessed her with the saving word of peace.

I love the fact that Scripture portrays Jesus mercifully connecting with the disenfranchised and marginalized people of his day and demonstrating the Father's heart of love for all His children.

Let us turn a few pages in this same Gospel to the story of Jesus' visit to Mary and Martha's house in chapter 10.

> *As Jesus and his disciples were on their way, he came to a village where a woman named Martha opened her home to him. She had a sister called Mary, who sat at the Lord's feet listening to what he said. But Martha was distracted by all the preparations that had to be made. She came to him and asked, "Lord, don't you care that my sister has left me to do the work by myself? Tell her to help me!" "Martha, Martha," the Lord answered, "you are worried and upset about many things, but few things are needed—or indeed only one. Mary has chosen what is better, and it will not be taken away from her." (John 10:38-42, NIV)*

During the time of Jesus, men of the community would often gather around the rabbi to hear his teachings. In this passage, Mary crashed the men's meeting and positioned herself, uninvited, in their midst. In response, Jesus not only pushed aside the cultural assumption that a woman could not sit at a rabbi's feet, he also commended Mary's desire to spend time with him. According to Jesus, Mary's desire to rest in his presence and receive his teaching was more important than Martha's conformity to the "rules" of the day. This is certainly a strong testimony of his desire to engage all of us, men and women, in that place of intimacy.

It is worthy to note that the Gospel of Luke also mentions women in the crowd of Jesus' followers. In Luke 8, we read:

> *After this, Jesus traveled about from one town and village to another, proclaiming the good news of the kingdom of God. The Twelve were with him, and also some women who had been cured of evil spirits and diseases: Mary (called Magdalene) from whom seven demons had come out; Joanna the wife of Chuza, the manager of Herod's household; Susanna; and many others. These women were helping to support them out of their own means. (Luke 8:1-3, NIV)*

In Jesus' time, it would have been atypical of rabbis to have female followers. Furthermore, it is significant that these women contributed from their own resources to support Jesus' ministry. It is also worth noting that while only one male disciple remained with Jesus at the cross, there were several women from among his followers who endured observing his crucifixion. Then, these women followed up by going to the tomb on Sunday to finish preparing his body for burial after all the male disciples had fled in fear.

I must include the story of the woman caught in adultery here, because it harmonizes so well with what we know about Jesus.

> *At dawn he appeared again in the temple courts, where all the people gathered around him, and he sat down to teach them. The teachers of the law and the Pharisees brought in a woman caught in adultery. They made her stand before the group and said to Jesus, "Teacher, this woman was caught in the act of adultery. In the Law Moses commanded us to stone such women. Now what do you say?" They were using this question as a trap, in order to*

> have a basis for accusing him.
>
> But Jesus bent down and started to write on the ground with his finger. When they kept on questioning him, he straightened up and said to them, 'Let any one of you who is without sin be the first to throw a stone at her.' Again he stooped down and wrote on the ground. At this, those who heard began to go away one at a time, the older ones first, until only Jesus was left, with the woman still standing there.
>
> Jesus straightened up and asked her, "Woman, where are they? Has no one condemned you?" "No one, sir," she said. "Then neither do I condemn you," Jesus declared. "Go now and leave your life of sin." (John 8:2-11, NIV)

Though the Law penalizes both men and women for adultery, in this case the Pharisees, intent on trying to trap Jesus, only seemed interested in punishing the woman. Regardless, Jesus again extended mercy in a situation where a woman faced imminent death. He not only refused to speak condemnation, but sent her away forgiven with a simple admonition to sin no more.

One final passage of note is the account of the first witness of Jesus' resurrection found in John 20.

> Now Mary stood outside the tomb crying. As she wept, she bent over to look into the tomb and saw two angels in white, seated where Jesus' body had been, one at the head and the other at the foot. They asked her, "Woman, why are you crying?" "They have taken my Lord away," she said, "and I don't know where they have put him."
>
> At this, she turned around and saw Jesus standing there, but she did not realize that it was Jesus. He asked her, "Woman, why are you crying? Who is it you are looking for?" Thinking he was

> *the gardener, she said, "Sir, if you have carried him away, tell me where you have put him, and I will get him." Jesus said to her, "Mary."*
>
> *She turned toward him and cried out in Aramaic, "Rabboni!" (which means "Teacher"). Jesus said, "Do not hold on to me, for I have not yet ascended to the Father. Go instead to my brothers and tell them, I am ascending to my Father and your Father, to my God and your God."*
>
> *Mary Magdalene went to the disciples with the news: "I have seen the Lord!" And she told them that he had said these things to her.* (John 20:11-18, NIV)

In a time when women were not allowed to testify in court because they were considered "unreliable witnesses", God chose a woman of questionable reputation to be the first eyewitness of Jesus' resurrection. In His wisdom, God entrusted the Gospel to one whom society deemed untrustworthy, and in doing so demonstrated the value and role of women in His Kingdom. The disciples, reflecting the attitudes of the day, initially did not believe Mary's testimony, but for Mary this hardly mattered. Jesus had spoken to her directly, saying that His Father was her Father and His God was her God.

Each of these interactions gives us insight into the heart of Jesus. He included women in situations and conversations where they normally would not have been welcomed. He valued their worship as well as their evangelism. He pushed against the cultural norms of the Hebrew culture and honored them with dignity. His actions, as well as his attitude, demonstrate that women belong alongside men, whether in public or private settings, as full participants in the Kingdom of God.

THE OTHER HALF OF THE ARMY

Fourth Chapter

NEW COVENANT PERSPECTIVES

Jesus' influence and Spirit-inspired interpretations of prophecy had an impact on the apostles' understanding of women and their role, not only in the Kingdom and the church, but in culture and society as well. Consider that following the ascension of Jesus, during the waiting period prior to Pentecost, women were present at early Acts church gatherings.

> *When they arrived, they went upstairs to the room where they were staying. Those present were Peter, John, James and Andrew; Philip and Thomas, Bartholomew and Matthew; James son of Alphaeus and Simon the Zealot, and Judas son of James. They all joined together constantly in prayer, along with the women and Mary the mother of Jesus, and with his brothers. (Acts 1:13-14, NIV)*

Then, consider the Scripture which the Spirit brought to Peter's mind as he preached his first sermon on the day of Pentecost in Acts 2.

> *"No, this is what was spoken by the prophet Joel: In the last days, God says, 'I will pour out my Spirit on all people. Your sons and daughters will prophesy, your young men will see visions, your old men will dream dreams. Even on my servants, both men and women, I will pour out my Spirit in those days, and they will prophesy.'"* (Acts 2:16-18, NIV)

By quoting a prophecy from the second chapter of Joel, Peter explained to the crowd what they were experiencing on the day of Pentecost. The odd sound of wind, strange manifestations of fire and people speaking in languages they had never learned was certainly cause for confusion, but Joel's prophecy provided at least a partial explanation. Take note that in this outpouring of the Spirit of God there are no distinctions of gender, age or class. Instead, God gives His Spirit to anyone who turns to Him in faith. Throughout the development of the early church, that attitude of total inclusivity was not only maintained but was taught as well. We shall see this more as we look at Scripture, particularly the book of Acts.

Before moving forward, let me add a comment concerning Acts 1:14 and the word translated as brothers. The word in Greek is *adelphoi*, a plural word referring to siblings in a family. In New Testament usage, depending on the context, *adelphoi* may refer to men (brothers) or to both men and women who are siblings (brothers and sisters) in God's family, the church. I make this point for a couple of reasons. First, as we will explore later, English translations can be slanted to reflect a more male perspective. Let me clarify that I am not in any way suggesting we play around with how we translate passages speaking about God. God is triune, Father, Son and Holy Spirit and it is important for us to maintain those understandings. All of our attempts to anthropomorphize God are in some respect placing limitations on the infinite, eternally existent Creator, but they do help us understand more about Him. He has chosen to reveal Himself to us both through the inspiration of His Word and through the incarnation as His Son. However, there are many reasons for us to expand our understanding of passages about the church and the family of God as we consider our sisters in the Lord.

There are compelling reasons for us who are male leaders in particular to consider a more inclusive use of language. At any given church gathering, with the exception of men's meetings, it is more than likely that a majority of the crowd will be women. When we teach, preach or read Scripture aloud and use only male pronouns or male-oriented translations, we are essentially excluding our sisters in Christ from consideration. That may not be our heart or our intent, but with very little effort we can take the time to make women feel included. For far too long they have been treated as second-class citizens and given no real voice. They should be treated with all the honor and respect due them as citizens of God's Kingdom, free from any attitude or action that leaves them feeling oppressed or under-valued. Therefore it can be helpful, particularly in church settings, to use a translation of Scripture that uses more inclusive language. The newest edition of the New International Version (2011, Biblia) and the New Living Translation, for the most part, do an excellent job maintaining contextual integrity, while using more inclusive phrasing, like translating *adelphoi* as brothers and sisters.

Let me speak briefly to the phrase "sons of God" which shows up with some frequency in the New Testament literature. Consider Paul's use of it in Galatians 4.

> *But when the set time had fully come, God sent his Son, born of a woman, born under the law, to redeem those under the law, that we might receive adoption to sonship. Because you are his sons, God sent the Spirit of his Son into our hearts, the Spirit who calls out, "Abba, Father." So you are no longer a slave, but God's child; and since you are his child, God has made you also an heir. (Galatians 4:4-7, NIV)*

In the newest NIV translation (2011), a footnote for the phrase "adoption to sonship" reads, "the Greek word for adoption to sonship is a legal term referring to the full legal standing of an adopted male heir in Roman culture." It is similar to the declaration of a Jewish father declaring over his child at a Bar Mitzvah, "this is my beloved son, in whom I am well pleased." The phrase is a recognition of full status within the family and a readiness to take over the family business. In this sense, women should welcome adoption as sons, for it means that all the rights and privileges that any male child might receive belong to them as well. I am always mindful of the fact that I, as a male, am identified as part of the bride of Christ, but I can think of no more important union for me to celebrate. However, if we want women to be comfortable being called sons, it should be in the right context with the full meaning explained.

Let us look at several more passages that speak of women and their roles in the early church. From the book of Acts, we see that Paul placed no gender restrictions on his attacks against the early followers of Jesus. Consider Acts 9.

> *Meanwhile, Saul was still breathing out murderous threats against the Lord's disciples. He went to the high priest and asked him for letters to the synagogues in Damascus, so that if he found any there who belonged to the Way, whether men or women, he might take them as prisoners to Jerusalem. Acts 9:1-2 (NIV)*

In Saul's mind, it was just as important to stop women from spreading the good news as it was to stop men. This is significant. Women were not generally considered a threat, since their testimony was not considered worthwhile. Remember that they felt no fear in staying at the crucifixion long after the other disciples had fled.

We have already looked at the Spirit being poured out on "all flesh" in Acts 2, so it is helpful to see how that played out beyond Pentecost. Clearly, both men and women assumed all sorts of leadership roles in the early church. Consider Paul's letter to the Roman church in chapter 16 where he honorably mentions 29 co-laborers at the close of his letter. Of the 29, 10 are women, notably Phoebe, who is called a deacon and a person of influence (perhaps even translating *prostatis* as "presiding officer.")[1] In verse 7, there is mention of Andronicus and Junia (please note that the name is definitely feminine in the most reliable manuscripts) who are described as outstanding among the apostles. That verse has obviously given some translators problems since some versions have changed the name to be masculine (Junias) even though there is no historical or exegetical evidence for Junia to have been a man. Clearly, Paul has no problem expressing thanks to this woman for her apostolic leadership. Further, we have Chloe (1 Corinthians 1:11) and Nympha (Colossians 4:15) who are mentioned as leaders of churches, most likely house churches that met in their homes.

---

1 In the ESV, *prostatis* is translated as "patron," so that verse 2 reads "she has been a patron of many and of myself as well."

Paul mentions a pair of women in Philippians 4:2, Euodia and Syntyche, whom he calls "fellow workers," who contended alongside him in the sharing of the Gospel message.

Other women mentioned in the New Testament are: Philip's daughters (Acts 21:9), Priscilla (Acts 18:26; Romans 16:3-5, etc.), Apphia (Philemon 2), "the chosen lady" (2 John 1), "the chosen sister" (2 John 13), and possibly Lydia (Acts 16:40). Just as there have been good and bad male leaders, there were good and bad female leaders. Sadly, the church in Thyatira was being corrupted by the teachings and false prophecies of a wicked and immoral female leader (Revelation 2:20-24), as was, it seems, the church in Ephesus (1 Timothy 1:3-4, cf. 2:12), which we'll look at more closely later.

It is worthwhile to note Paul's early thinking about this matter. It is generally accepted by scholars that Galatians represents one of the earliest New Testament documents written, probably penned in 49 AD. In it, Paul takes the time to write about the overall inclusiveness of the Gospel he has been preaching. In chapter 3 we read:

> *So in Christ Jesus you are all children of God through faith, for all of you who were baptized into Christ have clothed yourselves with Christ. There is neither Jew nor Gentile, neither slave nor free, nor is there male and female, for you are all one in Christ Jesus. (Galatians 3:6-28, NIV)*

There are no distinctions of race, class or gender by which any individual can claim superiority over another. The playing field has been forever leveled by the finished work of the Cross. Dr. N. T. Wright, in his conference paper "Women's Service in the

Church," delivered at St. John's College in September of 2004, had this to add about this important passage.

> "So does Paul mean that in Christ the created order itself is undone? Is he saying, as some have suggested, that we go back to a kind of chaos in which no orders of creation apply any longer? Or is he saying that we go on, like the Gnostics, from the first rather shabby creation in which silly things like gender-differentiation apply to a new world in which we can all live as hermaphrodites – which, again, some have suggested, and which has interesting possible ethical spin-offs? No. Paul is a theologian of new creation, and it is always the renewal and reaffirmation of the existing creation, never its denial, as not only Galatians 6.16 but also of course Romans 8 and 1 Corinthians 15 make so very clear. Indeed, Genesis 1—3 remains enormously important for Paul throughout his writings."

> "What then is he saying? Remember that he is controverting in particular those who wanted to enforce Jewish regulations, and indeed Jewish ethnicity, upon Gentile converts. Remember the synagogue prayer in which the man who prays thanks God that he has not made him a Gentile, a slave or a woman – at which point the women in the congregation thank God 'that you have made me according to your will'. I think Paul is deliberately marking out the family of Abraham reformed in the Messiah as a people who cannot pray that prayer, since within this family these distinctions are now irrelevant."

One last powerful example of the shift brought on by Jesus and his inauguration of new covenant realities is the sign of the new covenant. Whereas under the old covenant, the sign of circumcision was restricted to Jewish males, the new covenant sign of baptism is gender inclusive. Paul makes this point clearly in Colossians.

> *In him you were also circumcised with a circumcision not performed by human hands. Your whole self, ruled by the flesh was put off when you were circumcised by Christ, having been buried with him in baptism, in which you were also raised with him through your faith in the working of God, who raised him from the dead. When you were dead in your sins and in the uncircumcision of your flesh, God made you alive with Christ. He forgave us all our sins, having cancelled the charge of our legal indebtedness, which stood against us and condemned us; he has taken it away, nailing it to the cross. (Colossians 2:11-14, NIV)*

Every single one of us who follows Christ through the waters of baptism, male or female, child or adult, regardless of race has erected a signpost marking our identification with His death and resurrection, as well as a clear representation of our inclusion in the family as His children with all the ensuing rights and privileges.

THE BARRIERS OF CHURCH TRADITION

We have already considered that there is a strong spiritual component to the longstanding, global oppression of women. The enemy of our souls understood from the protevangelion, the first mention of the Gospel (Genesis 3:15), that his undoing would come from a child born of woman. And that component, unfortunately, has been taken on and enhanced throughout history even by many male leaders in the church. I put forth some quotes from significant names in our own history for consideration.[2]

> "Praise be to God that he has not created me a Gentile, a woman or a hog."
>
> Hebrew Prayer

---

[2] To read more quotes see: Gene Edwards, *The Christian Woman...Set Free.* (Jacksonville, FL; Seedsowers, 2005).

"Woman is a temple built over a sewer. It is contrary to the order of nature and of the law for women to speak in a gathering."

St. Jerome

"To make women learned and to make a fox tame work out to the same end. Educating a woman or a fox simply makes them more cunning."

King James

There were strong misogynistic feelings in the hearts of some very important leaders of influence in our Christian history. And while they may have been only reflecting the historical and cultural influences of their day, these men had significant influence through their writings and, in the case of Jerome, Bible translation. The Latin Vulgate is attributed to him and was the single most influential translation of the Scriptures prior to the King James. It has had at least some bearing on every translation since.

I will give two examples of how Jerome's view of women surfaced as he translated. In a verse we have already looked at, Genesis 3:6, many of our translations say:

> When the woman saw that the fruit of the tree was good for food and pleasing to the eye, and also desirable for gaining wisdom, she took some and ate it. She also gave some to her husband, who was with her, and he ate it.

Jerome in his Latin vulgate left out a single Hebrew word: *im*.[3] This omission of the word translated as "who was with her" means Eve is alone to make the decision to eat the fruit, making her more at

---

3 (*Prop.* conjunction, communion; *adv.* together, moreover, at the same time). H.W.F. Gesenius. *Gesenius' Hebrew and Chaldee lexicon to the Old Testament Scriptures.* (Bellingham, WA: Logos Bible Software, 1979).

blame for the fall of humanity. As I said, the Latin Vulgate has remained a very important translation. It is particularly disconcerting that a very well known English translation, the Revised Standard, also omits this important phrase, leaving readers to believe that Adam was not with her as she chose to eat.

Another very important alteration to the text is made by Jerome in Genesis 3:16. God had been addressing the serpent in the garden with severe words, and he finished his warning to Eve saying: "Your desire will be for your husband, and he will rule over you." While "he will rule over you" makes clear the husband's predominance over the wife, the impact should be counterbalanced by the other half of the verse, "your desire will be for your husband," which, as we saw earlier, connotes a nuance of the wife's control of her husband. In Jerome's version, however, that half of the verse is eliminated. Instead, Jerome wrote "you will be under the power of your husband and he will rule over you," prescribing complete subjection and subordination for the woman as a divine mandate.

I maintain that a strong male hierarchical lens has colored some of our more popular modern Bible translations and that this filter does not reflect the true nature of God's heart toward women. At the extreme, this distortion of Scripture has been used to defend the psychological, emotional and even physical abuse of women. It represents Scripture manipulation at its worst.

We should be wary of following after the traditions of our forebears simply because it has always been done that way. Jesus has harsh words when our traditions contravene the heart of God. In Mark chapter 7, he addresses those concerns to the Pharisees.

> *The Pharisees and some of the teachers of the law who had come from Jerusalem gathered around Jesus and saw some of his disciples eating food with hands that were defiled, that is, unwashed. (The Pharisees and all the Jews do not eat unless they give their hands a ceremonial washing, holding to the tradition of the elders. When they come from the marketplace they do not eat unless they wash. And they observe many other traditions, such as the washing of cups, pitchers and kettles.)*
>
> *So the Pharisees and teachers of the law asked Jesus, "Why don't your disciples live according to the tradition of the elders instead of eating their food with defiled hands?" He replied, "Isaiah was right when he prophesied about you hypocrites; as it is written:*
>
> *'These people honor me with their lips, but their hearts are far from me. They worship me in vain; their teachings are merely human rules.'*
>
> *You have let go of the commands of God and are holding on to human traditions." And he continued, "You have a fine way of setting aside the commands of God in order to observe your own traditions! For Moses said, 'Honor your father and mother,' and, 'Anyone who curses their father or mother is to be put to death.' But you say that if anyone declares that what might have been used to help their father or mother is Corban (that is, devoted to God)—then you no longer let them do anything for their father or mother. Thus you nullify the word of God by your tradition that you have handed down. And you do many things like that." (Mark 7:1-13, NIV)*

It behooves us when we read such warnings to safeguard that we haven't hung our theological hats on traditions which won't stand up against the larger revelation of God's heart in Scripture. I am well aware there are a few places in Paul's writings which seem to give fuel to the argument for restricting women from church leadership, but I will maintain that some of our interpretation of those verses has been biased by long-standing traditions of men, some with a very low view of women. I will address each of those pericopes, these self-contained portions of Scripture, beginning in the next chapter.

Fifth Chapter

CHALLENGING PASSAGES

As we review the passages typically quoted to defend exclusive male leadership, I am reminded of a statement made by Peter.

> *Bear in mind that our Lord's patience means salvation, just as our dear brother Paul also wrote you with the wisdom that God gave him. He writes the same way in all his letters, speaking in them of these matters. His letters contain some things that are hard to understand, which ignorant and unstable people distort, as they do the other Scriptures, to their own destruction. (2 Peter 3:15-16, NIV)*

I quote this because the ensuing passages come from Paul's letters. To some extent I have already demonstrated Paul's positive attitude toward women, so how is it that we find these seemingly restrictive thoughts from the same pen? Paul is not of two minds, and Scripture does not contain contradictions. So what are we to do?

Since our understanding of key verses of Scripture will influence our ultimate understanding, it is important to address those passages exegetically. For those unfamiliar with the term, exegesis involves an examination of a passage to determine first and foremost what the author intended to communicate to the original readers. Many factors need to be considered such as grammar (in the cases I will be addressing, we'll be looking at the original Greek language and grammar), vocabulary, literary and historical context as well as cultural issues and concerns. Attempting to cross the divide between two languages, in this case from first century Koine Greek to 21st century English, while maintaining the same or similar meanings presents a huge challenge. However, tackling passages exegetically and examining the culture, language and local situations Paul was addressing may help us make sense of some apparent contradictions. For the sake of simplicity, we will look at the passages in canonical order.

The passages in question are: 1 Corinthians 11:2-19, 1 Corinthians 14:34-35, Ephesians 5:15-27, 1 Timothy 2:9-15, 1 Timothy 3:1-7 and 1 Timothy 3:8-12.

I will include the full text from the NIV (2011 edition) for all of these passages, but will add comments and suggest other translations when, in my opinion, they represent Paul's intent more accurately. Please note that my opinions are based on much personal study of Scripture, as well as commentaries and writings of others. I do not pretend to have the final word on the text, but I believe with continued study from all parts of the body of Christ, we can achieve deeper understanding of what these passages entail.

1 CORINTHIANS 11:2-19

Part of the challenge in exegetical work is determining author's intent. For example, in 1 Corinthians 11, I believe Paul is addressing questions raised in a letter from the church in Corinth. We see the evidence in chapter 7, verse 1. There, we read the following: "Now for the matters you wrote about: 'It is good for a man not to have sexual relations with a woman.'" At first glance it might appear that Paul recommends a total physical separation of the sexes, but in fact he is addressing a concern about which the church in Corinth had written. We discern this because he goes on in chapter 7 to address sexual intimacy in the context of marriage, therefore he cannot mean to suggest complete abstinence in all circumstances as it initially appears in verse 1. From this we can surmise that from time to time, Paul quotes from the Corinthians' letter. The problem for us, as 21st century readers, and for translators, is that we do not have a copy of the letter they wrote. So, there are times when we must use our contextual considerations, grammatical analysis and best judgment to determine whether Paul is quoting the Corinthians or writing originally. The 1 Corinthians 11 passage is particularly difficult, representing what is, at best, a very murky portion of the letter from the church to Paul. It reads:

> ²*I praise you for remembering me in everything and for holding to the traditions just as I passed them on to you.* ³*But I want you to realize that the head of every man is Christ, and the head of the woman is man, and the head of Christ is God.* ⁴*Every man who prays or prophesies with his head covered dishonors his head.* ⁵*But every woman who prays or prophesies with her head uncovered dishonors her head—it is the same as having her head shaved.* ⁶*For if a woman does not cover her head, she might as well have her hair cut off; but if it is a disgrace for a woman to have her hair cut off or her head shaved, then she should cover her head.*

> [7] *A man ought not to cover his head, since he is the image and glory of God; but woman is the glory of man.* [8] *For man did not come from woman, but woman from man;* [9] *neither was man created for woman, but woman for man.* [10] *It is for this reason that a woman ought to have authority over her own head, because of the angels.* [11] *Nevertheless, in the Lord woman is not independent of man, nor is man independent of woman.* [12] *For as woman came from man, so also man is born of woman. But everything comes from God.*
>
> [13] *Judge for yourselves: Is it proper for a woman to pray to God with her head uncovered?* [14] *Does not the very nature of things teach you that if a man has long hair, it is a disgrace to him,* [15] *but that if a woman has long hair, it is her glory? For long hair is given to her as a covering.* [16] *If anyone wants to be contentious about this, we have no other practice—nor do the churches of God.*
>
> [17] *In the following directives I have no praise for you, for your meetings do more harm than good.* [18] *In the first place, I hear that when you come together as a church, there are divisions among you, and to some extent I believe it.* [19] *No doubt there have to be differences among you to show which of you have God's approval.* (1 Corinthians 11: 2-19, NIV)

In this passage, we glimpse Paul's sense of the interdependency between men and women. Most translations and commentators agree Paul is not talking about the marriage relationship in verse 3, where he says that man is the head of the woman, because he is addressing what constitutes appropriate behavior and decorum during public worship. Nor is he establishing a chain of command since he is clearly using the word head (*kephalē* in the Greek) to mean "source" here. Several early church theologians attest to this. Athanasius, Bishop of Alexandria says in De Synodis Anathema:

"For the head (which is the source) of all things is the Son, but God is the head (which is the source) of Christ."

Cyril, who was Archbishop of Alexandria wrote in his De Recta Fide:

> "Therefore of our race he [Adam] became first head, which is source, and was of the earth and earthy. Since Christ was named the second Adam, he has been placed as head, which is source, of those who through Him have been formed anew unto Him unto immortality through sanctification in the Spirit. Therefore he himself our source, which is head, has appeared as a human being. Yet he, though God by nature, has himself a generating head, the heavenly Father, and he himself, though God according to his nature, yet being the Word, was begotten of him. Because head means source, he establishes the truth for those who are wavering in their mind that man is the head of woman, for she was taken out of him. Therefore as God according to his nature, the one Christ and Son and Lord has as his head the heavenly Father, having himself become our head because he is of the same stock according to the flesh."[1]

I will address this concept of headship further when we look at Ephesians 5, but it is very important for us to understand that Paul is not establishing any sort of hierarchy or chain of command in 1 Corinthians 11. If he were, we would have to ask if he is teaching some sort of hierarchy within the Trinity, and I am certain that was not the case.

In the passage, there are some gender issues related to how people are coifed when they come to church. It is worth noting that there is no word in the original Greek that can be translated "scarf or

---

1   I am grateful to the comprehensive study of Margaret Mowczko on this subject and owe these citations to her. http://newlife.id.au/equality-and-gender-issues/kephale-and-male-headship-in-pauls-letters/

head covering" in verses 5 and 6, so I believe Paul is talking about some culturally specific issues regarding how people wore their hair.[2] Of far greater importance is Paul's heart about the gender issue, which is found in the center of the passage.

> *It is for this reason that a woman ought to have authority over her own head, because of the angels. Nevertheless, in the Lord woman is not independent of man, nor is man independent of woman. For as woman came from man, so also man is born of woman. But everything comes from God. (1 Corinthians 11: 10-12)*

Obviously gender differences exist, but here Paul highlights that neither men nor women can claim superiority, since neither is independent of the other and both have their source in God. He directs the church to set aside their differences, lest there be division in the body of Christ, a theme which he has emphasized from the very start.

In verse 16, we find a potential translation challenge that, if left unattended, could alter our understanding of Paul's intent.

> *If anyone wants to be contentious about this, we have no other practice—nor do the churches of God.*

The word "other" is the Greek word *toioutos*, which fairly universally means such or like. So, Paul means to say that in the circle of churches with which he has affiliation, there is no such practice of making hair an issue over which to become divided. This appeal for unity in the church over hair length and style should easily translate to the greater need for us to be one body, men and women working with mutual respect for one another.

---

2 *The matter of head covering is not the focus of our study, so I will refrain from delving more into the subject here. Instead, I recommend a very helpful article on this subject, accessible online, published in the Priscilla Papers: Volume 20, Number 3, Summer 2006, called " Wild Hair and Gender Equality in 1 Corinthians 11:2-16" by Philip B. Payne.*

1 CORINTHIANS 14:34-35

1 Corinthians 14 is one of two passages used to suggest that women should not teach or speak in church. The New International Version reads:

> *Women should remain silent in the churches. They are not allowed to speak, but must be in submission, as the law says. If they want to inquire about something, they should ask their own husbands at home; for it is disgraceful for a woman to speak in the church. (1 Corinthians 14:34-35)*

At first blush, it truly feels like Paul is contradicting himself. He has just explained in detail how men and women should comport themselves in worship and utilize the gifts of the Spirit, some of which are dependent on speaking. In fact, chapter 14 opens with a declaration that all believers should earnestly desire spiritual gifts, especially the gift of prophecy. Unless Paul has suddenly changed his mind, verses 34 and 35 must mean something other than what they initially seem.

Let me posit a couple of alternatives. This could easily be another occasion when Paul is quoting from the Corinthians' original letter. While we do not have that letter for comparison, we can deduce that these two verses don't sound like Paul at all, especially the assertion for women to be in subjection "as the Law says." There is no such direct statement in the Law, although such a statement might be found in the Midrash (the rabbinical explanation and commentary on the law). Further, the text says "if they have a desire to learn," which directly contradicts 1 Timothy 2:11 where Paul writes the imperative command, "women must learn." From this, it seems Paul had a deep conviction that women should be present in the churches to receive teaching along with their male counterparts. Otherwise, it seems odd that he would reprimand women to silence. As we read on, it is essential to consider the context of the passage.

> *Or did the word of God originate with you? Or are you the only people it has reached? If anyone thinks they are a prophet or otherwise gifted by the Spirit, let them acknowledge that what I am writing to you is the Lord's command. But if anyone ignores this, they will themselves be ignored. Therefore, my brothers and sisters, be eager to prophesy, and do not forbid speaking in tongues. (1 Corinthians 14:36-39, NIV)*

Verse 36 begins with a particle in Greek, which could be translated in our day as, "What? Did this word come to you directly?"[3] If Paul indeed has been quoting a letter from Corinth in verses 34 and 35, and if he is as convicted by female participation as it seems in other parts of the New Testament, the remainder of this passage becomes clear: Paul strongly disagrees with the notion of women's silence in the church and instead declares that brothers and sisters (adelphoi) should eagerly prophesy and speak in tongues.

There is one other possible interpretation of the text we are examining. If the passage is examined lexicographically, we find that the word "speak" (*laleō*)[4] Paul uses here is actually a word commonly used for talking or chatting. It very well could have been that in this new cultural setting, where women were suddenly welcome to sit and engage with men (the church), Paul was admonishing against distracting chatter. In our day, we have a similar problem with cell phones and texting, much to the dismay of people who

---

3 ἤ *ē, ay; a prim. particle of distinction between two connected terms; disjunctive, or; comparative, than:—and, but (either), (n-) either, except it be, (n-) or (else), rather, save, than, that, what, yea.*

4 λαλέω: *to speak or talk, with the possible implication of more informal usage (though this cannot be clearly and consistently shown from New Testament contexts)—'to speak, to say, to talk, to tell.'* Louw-Nida

want to pay close attention to worship and preaching free from distraction. If Paul truly had wanted to forbid women from teaching and preaching, he had any number of more specific words he could have used.

My interpretive preference for 1 Corinthians 14 is the first alternative I identified. I am quite sure that Paul was not attempting to silence women in any formal way, particularly when he takes time to describe how women should dress when engaging in speaking activities in a worship setting and encourages them to prophesy and speak in tongues. Applying this to our modern setting, we too should eagerly encourage the active participation of women in ecclesial environments.

EPHESIANS 5

As I have looked at the various views on women and their roles within the church and ministry, other concerns have been raised in my discussions and study. Submission and headship are two concepts most often addressed in Christian circles when it comes to the role of women. Most, if not all, beliefs on submission and headship are born out of a few verses in Paul's teaching about marriage in Ephesians 5. For us to gain a full understanding of any series of verses, we often need to place them within the larger context of Scripture to see how they relate to God's nature and character. Submission is a very important concept, as it clearly underlies a proper understanding of covenant relationship, so we must analyze it properly by taking into account its broader context. Let us take a look at one of the key passages that talks about submission.

> *[18]And do not get drunk with wine, for that is debauchery, but be filled with the Spirit, [19]addressing one another in psalms and hymns and spiritual songs, singing and making melody to the Lord with your heart, [20]giving thanks always and for everything to God the Father in the name of our Lord Jesus Christ, [21]submitting to one another out of reverence for Christ. [22]Wives, submit to your own husbands, as to the Lord. [23]For the husband is the head of the wife even as Christ is the head of the church, his body, and is himself its Savior. [24]Now as the church submits to Christ, so also wives should submit in everything to their husbands. [25]Husbands, love your wives, as Christ loved the church and gave himself up for her, [26]that he might sanctify her, having cleansed her by the washing of water with the word, [27]so that he might present the church to himself in splendor, without spot or wrinkle or any such thing, that she might be holy and without blemish. [28]In the same way husbands should love their wives as their own bodies. He who loves his wife loves himself. [29]For no one ever hated his own flesh, but nourishes and cherishes it, just as Christ does the church, [30]because we are members of his body. [31]'Therefore a man shall leave his father and mother and hold fast to his wife, and the two shall become one flesh.' [32]This mystery is profound, and I am saying that it refers to Christ and the church. (Ephesians 5:18-32, ESV)*

For us to grasp the full meaning of Paul's instruction, we begin by looking at the greater context of the passage. Earlier in the chapter (although remember there were no chapters, verse numbers or paragraph headings when he wrote this letter), Paul told the Ephesian believers to imitate God. When I reflect on a command like that, I can easily feel overwhelmed. How could I possibly fulfill the expectation to model God in any meaningful way? But as Paul gives examples of what imitation could look like in the lives of ordinary believers, he offers the only possible solution to our dilemma. Verse 18 articulates it well: we must be filled with the Holy Spirit, our Helper, (see John 14:16 and 26) for any of this to work. In the Greek, the verb is a present passive imperative, meaning that it should be a continuous experience. All Greek verbs have these three components: tense, voice and mood, which help us to understand their meaning better. The imperative mood here reveals that to be filled with the Spirit is a command, not an optional task. We learn from Paul that we should regularly position ourselves, through relational intimacy with the Father, to be filled again with His Holy Spirit.

The apostle indicates what a Spirit-filled life looks like in relationship. People who are living a life full of Holy Spirit will exhibit these characteristics: they will speak positively, sing joyously, thank God, and practice mutual submission because of their love for Jesus. Mutual submission as in verse 21, is a common theme for Paul and is reflected elsewhere in Scripture. For example, in Ephesians we find these words, "Be kind and compassionate to one another, forgiving each other, just as in Christ God forgave you." (Ephesians 4:32, NIV) In Romans 12:10 we read, "Be devoted to one another in love. Honor one another above yourselves." (NIV) Please note the phrase "one another" in these passages. There should be a mutual understanding among the parties involved or the relationship will suffer. Consider his words in Philippians.

> *Do nothing out of selfish ambition or vain conceit. Rather, in humility value others above yourselves, not looking to your own interests but each of you to the interests of the others. (Philippians 2:3-4, NIV)*

And then, from the letter to the Colossians,

> *Therefore, as God's chosen people, holy and dearly loved, clothe yourselves with compassion, kindness, humility, gentleness and patience. (Colossians 3:12, NIV)*

As Paul writes about relationships, he emphasizes the importance of unselfishness. When he comes to the marriage relationship, he stresses the value of submission even further. I like to divide the word into two parts to help remind myself what submission means. If I take off the "sub", which means "under" and then apply that to "mission", I realize that to submit is to come under another person to support their mission. A good biblical example of this is when Aaron and Hur held up Moses' arms so that Israel would continue to battle favorably against the Amalekites (see Exodus 17:8-13).

Let me speak a little more about the grammar found in Ephesians 5, particularly verses 21 and 22. The verb to submit is a participle in the original language, used to describe someone or something in the same fashion that an adjective would be used (i.e. submitting). In verse 22, contrary to what we find in many of our English translations, the verb is neither repeated, nor is it found in the imperative mood. That structure in the Greek is called an ellipsis, the missing word being understood from the form which came before. It could be better understood to say, "Submitting to one another out of the fear of Christ, wives to your husbands as to the Lord." There is no paragraph heading to isolate this as a concern for husbands and wives, so should be seen as a parenthetical to what Paul has just written. This mutual submission he mentions in verse 21 should also be reflected within the context of marriage. The same grammatical construction appears again in verse 24, "Now as the church submits to Christ, so also wives should submit to their husbands in everything" (NIV). The verb is again understood (an ellipsis) in the second part of the verse. It literally reads, "Now as the church submits to Christ, so wives to their husbands in everything." In the culture Paul was addressing, with Hellenism and its degrading and repressive view of women saturating much of the Roman Empire, I believe his command to husbands to love their wives in verse 25 (it is indeed a command in the form of a present, active, imperative verb) carries much more weight. It is clearly stated as a requirement with the addendum that a man should love his wife both as Christ loved the church and as he loves his own body. Consider by contrast for a moment some of the pervading thought of Greek philosophy from Aristotle. In "The Politics" he flatly declares, "as regards the sexes, the male is by nature superior and the female inferior, the male ruler and the female subject." This was the cultural environment into which the apostle was speaking; Paul was certainly sharing from a counter-cultural Kingdom perspective.

We cannot move forward without addressing the word Paul uses for "head" in these passages. As I mentioned earlier in our discussion of 1 Corinthians 11, we are faced again with the challenge of crossing the divide between languages, culture and history. In English, the word head often refers to one in charge, a leader or a boss, so many have concluded that Paul intends to show that the husband is the leader over the wife. In fact, in medieval Greek, the word *kephalē* can refer to a leader, especially when it is used a military setting. Our New Testament was not written in Medieval Greek, however, but in an earlier version of Greek called Koine, the language that was very widely used and understood in the first century. Much recent scholarship has challenged that meaning of the word in Scripture and rendered it as "source" instead.[5] Based on the most reliable lexicon for ancient Greek meaning, Liddel, Scott and Jones, I feel that 'source' is the correct understanding because I see how Paul used the word elsewhere, particularly in Colossians.

> *He (Christ) is also head (kephalē) of the body, the church; and He is the beginning (archē) the firstborn from the dead, so that He Himself will come to have first place in everything. (Colossians 1:18, NASB)*

Here Paul uses two words for head, *kephalē* which means source and archē which often refers to one who leads. Another passage where kephalē is used as source is in 1 Corinthians 11:3, as we have already seen.

> *But I want you to understand that Christ is the head of every man, and the man is the head of a woman, and God is the head of Christ. (1 Corinthians 11:3, NASB)*

The New Living Translation even suggests the following translation in its footnote: But, I want you to know: The source of every man is Christ, the source of woman is man, and the source of Christ is God. That particular verse helps us to look at this word from a different angle. I thank Danny Silk from Bethel Church in Redding, California for asking this question in one of his messages: What does it mean for God to be the head of Christ? Does that place restrictions on Jesus in any way? If Jesus is the head of the church, does that mean there is something the church can't do? No, Paul is speaking of Jesus being the firstborn of the Spirit, modeling for the church to become like its head, its source.

---

[5] For further reading, I suggest Manfred Brauch, *Abusing Scripture: The Consequences of Misreading the Bible* (Downers Grove, IL: InterVarsity Press, 2009).

A stronger justification for translating *kephalē* as source is to see how it is used in the Septuagint (LXX), the Greek translation of the Old Testament. As I noted earlier, Greek was the lingua franca of the culture in Jesus' day, and since many could not understand the Old Testament in its original Hebrew, it was translated into Greek. In the Septuagint, there is a tendency to translate Hebrew words literally. *Kephalē* (head) was rarely used to translate the Hebrew word "head" when it meant superior rank. The word used in those contexts would be *archē*. Further, if you look at the early Greek lexicons, none of them lists "head" as implying authority (see Liddell, Scott & Jones, Moulton and Milligan and S. C. Woodhouse for example). Rather as the citation in LSJ (945) says, "source" is an established metaphorical meaning of head. Even extra-biblical sources from the same time period, such as Philo in The Preliminary Studies, use it in that fashion: "of all the members of the clan here described Esau is the progenitor, the head of the whole creature." There is much more lexicographic data available, but I simply want to suggest that we should not hang the idea of husbandly authority on an unsubstantiated definition of *kephalē*. Linguistically, I am far more comfortable with the perspective that Christ is the sustainer and source of nurture for the church, and that, accordingly, the husband fulfills those same functions for his wife.

Many translators equate submission with obedience, but if Paul had wanted to convey that stronger meaning he undoubtedly would have used a different word. It would have been easy to use *hypakouō*, as he does shortly thereafter in Ephesians 6:1 and 5 in his instructions to children and slaves. The word for submit, however is *hypotassō*, which quite literally can mean to come along side one's mission as in the process of increasing understanding or receiving from and partnering with one another. Catherine Kroeger notes that when this verb is used in its opposite sense *(anupotassō)*, it was meant "to designate individuals who were not integrated into the group, dissociated from others, confused or difficult to comprehend. By contrast, he (Polybius) sometimes used *hupotassō* to indicate associations or relationships that led to greater understanding."[6]

In the only verse where this verb (submit) is used in the imperative mood (a command), Colossians 3:18, "Wives, submit yourselves to your husbands, as is fitting in the Lord," is found in the middle voice. When the middle voice is used in Greek, it places responsibility for action on the subject, in this case, the wives. With that understanding we see that this represents voluntary action on the part of wives. Nowhere does the New Testament speak of the husband having the right to demand submission from his wife. In fact, if we men are to take Paul seriously, we should regularly be on our knees before the Lord asking for assistance to love our wives in the same way Christ loved the church. In his excellent book, *What Paul Really Said About Women*, John Bristow notes that in the Ephesians passage Paul uses only 47 words to address women, while 143 words are directed at husbands.

I revisit this point (that there is no actual command for wives to submit) because the verses in Ephesians 5 in particular have been used to excuse, and even defend, both psychological and physical abuse of women. There is much evidence that church leaders have even told wives who have asked for protection from abusive husbands that they should submit to their husbands' behavior in order

---

6 Kroeger, Catherine. *Women, Abuse, and the Bible: How Scripture Can Be Used to Hurt or to Heal.* (Christians for Biblical Equality, 1988). Excerpted in http://www.rethinkingfaith.com/post/3350432647/kroeger-submission.

to be truly obedient to the Bible's commands. I find such advice to be unconscionable and I can find no evidence in Scripture where such behavior is acceptable. On the contrary, I believe it is the duty of men to protect women and that appropriate action should be taken to remove women caught in cycles of domestic abuse.

A further example from Paul's thinking, which I believe reflects his true thoughts about decision making for married couples, is his answer to the Corinthians' question about sexual intimacy found in 1 Corinthians.

> *The husband should fulfill his marital duty to his wife, and likewise the wife to her husband. The wife does not have authority over her own body but yields it to her husband. In the same way, the husband does not have authority over his own body but yields it to his wife. Do not deprive each other except perhaps by mutual consent and for a time, so that you may devote yourselves to prayer. Then come together again so that Satan will not tempt you because of your lack of self-control. (1 Corinthians 7:3-5, NIV)*

I find it significant that in the very sensitive matter of intimacy, Paul gives no advantage to either partner, and in fact says that each partner must yield authority over his or her body to the other. He even goes so far as to say that if there should be any abstention from sexual intimacy, the decision to abstain must only be made by mutual consent.

Broadening this point, the question is often asked, "What if the couple can't come to agreement?" My response is that if the two are indeed a one-flesh union and both are seeking guidance from the Holy Spirit, on any matter of decision-making, they should continue to pray, both individually and corporately, until a single answer of agreement is reached.

I have one final thought in the matter of equal standing for partners in a marriage. Consider what Paul writes to Timothy.

> *So I counsel younger widows to marry, to have children, to manage their homes and to give the enemy no opportunity for slander. (1 Timothy 5:14, NIV)*

In very strong language, Paul suggests that Timothy encourage young widows to remarry. The word he uses for "to manage a home" is a potent one *(oikodespoteō)*, used only one time in all the New Testament. The NASB translates the word as "keep house," but that weakens the meaning of this particular word. According to the Little Kittel, a New Testament Theological Dictionary, it means "to direct or be the master of a household." Compare that to the admonition to men in their qualifications list for leadership in 1 Timothy 3:4 where they are told to be good managers of their households. This is a different word *(proistēmi)* which is more accurately translated "to put before," "to present," or, in the intransitive middle, "to go before," "to preside," and figuratively "to surpass," "to lead," "to direct," "to assist," "to protect," "to represent," "to care for."⁷ I believe Paul sees both husbands and wives playing key partnership roles of leadership within families and households. It's not a battle of one-upmanship here, but rather a partnership committed to seeing God's purposes played out in every aspect of family living.

1 TIMOTHY 2:9-15

> *¹I urge, then, first of all, that petitions, prayers, intercession and thanksgiving be made for all people—²for kings and all those in authority, that we may live peaceful and quiet lives in all godliness and holiness. ³This is good, and pleases God our Savior, ⁴who*

---
7 Geoffrey W. Bromiley. *Theological Dictionary of the New Testament. (Grand Rapids, MI: W.B. Eerdmans, 1985).*

wants all people to be saved and to come to a knowledge of the truth. ⁵For there is one God and one mediator between God and mankind, the man Christ Jesus, ⁶who gave himself as a ransom for all people. This has now been witnessed to at the proper time. ⁷And for this purpose I was appointed a herald and an apostle—I am telling the truth, I am not lying—and a true and faithful teacher of the Gentiles.

⁸Therefore I want the men everywhere to pray, lifting up holy hands without anger or disputing. ⁹I also want the women to dress modestly, with decency and propriety, adorning themselves, not with elaborate hairstyles or gold or pearls or expensive clothes, ¹⁰but with good deeds, appropriate for women who profess to worship God.

¹¹A woman should learn in quietness and full submission. ¹²I do not permit a woman to teach or to assume authority over a man; she must be quiet. ¹³For Adam was formed first, then Eve. ¹⁴And Adam was not the one deceived; it was the woman who was deceived and became a sinner. ¹⁵But women will be saved through childbearing—if they continue in faith, love and holiness with propriety. (1 Timothy 2:1-15, NIV)

This is Paul's apostolic admonition to his young charge, Timothy, and is no doubt the most quoted passage in defense of women being restricted from church leadership positions. At first glance, it appears straightforward, rendering us prone to employ a good exegetical rule: if the plain sense makes common sense, seek no other sense. The chief problem, however, is that this passage seems to contradict a great deal of what we've come to understand about the apostle in his other letters. Consider again Romans 16 with his many accolades to women leaders. When apparent contradicting views arise regarding a text, that's when we must dig deeper to search out the author's true intent.

As the chapter opens, Paul encourages Timothy to be forthright in his instructions to the Ephesian believers regarding prayer for leaders and unity in worship. Notice the use of the word "all" in verse 4 and 6. Then he includes some instructions to men and women about worship decorum in verses 8 to 10. With his emphasis on equal standing before the Lord, he is quite clear that the wealthier women should not be dressing so fancifully as to set themselves above the less advantaged women of the congregation.

Given the times in which Timothy was leading the church in Ephesus, verse 11 is a culture-changing command. He says, "Let a woman learn." Let us pause for a moment. This was a radical statement in first century culture, where women were accustomed to being excluded from public gatherings or completely separated from men. They were also discouraged from pursuing any traditional educational experiences. The minority of women who were encouraged to gain any sort of meaningful education were the courtesans[8] of the day so that they could engage their clients in entertaining conversation. So this command, again in the imperative mood, causes me to question how this passage should be understood. Timothy says that women should focus on learning. Learning was uncommon for women in the first century and, understandably, they may have had many questions as they received instruction from God's word. The command to learn quietly and obediently does not call for submission to men, but instead directs women to submit themselves in obedience to the Word of God.

A great deal has been written about verse 12 and there are times when it feels like people are reaching to make the text say something it does not. Paul uses a word here in the text *(epitrepō)*, which

---

8   Courtesans were prostitutes catering especially to wealthy or upper-class clients.

is used in a very specific way in the original language. The NIV translates the word as "permit" in the opening phrase. Upon examining its uses in the New Testament, it always indicates permission regarding a very specific set of circumstances; it is never used in a universal sense. For examples of how this word is used, look at Matthew 8:21, where a disciple wants to be permitted to bury his father; Luke 8:32, where the demons want permission to enter the herd of pigs; Acts 26:1, where Paul is given permission to speak on his own behalf. So it would follow that in Timothy 5, Paul is addressing a specific situation that existed in the church at Ephesus and is not making a universal declaration.

The second major concern we need to address is the verb that Paul uses for "having authority." Most often Paul uses the word *exousia* for authority, which appears 25 times throughout his letters. However, in 1 Timothy 2 he uses the word *authenteō*. This should raise a red flag for the reader, prompting us to ask, why did he choose to use this particular word? God has spoken to us very clearly in his word and through the Spirit, inspiring the biblical writers as they wrote. Consequently, I do not believe that any word is used arbitrarily. In fact, this instance is the only time this word is used in all the New Testament. When a word is used only once in all of Scripture, it can be helpful to use extra-biblical sources to make sure we have an accurate understanding of its meaning. We must be careful not to weight a single word too heavily, since we don't think and communicate in single words but in full thoughts, whole sentences, and often complete paragraphs. Context will often help, but we should make sure to look at an author's overall intent to see how culture may have influenced what is being said. Let us begin by looking at why Paul wrote this particular letter to Timothy. We find a reason clearly stated in 1 Timothy, chapter one

> ³As I urged you when I went into Macedonia, stay there in Ephesus so that you may command certain people not to teach false doctrines any longer ⁴or to devote themselves to myths and endless genealogies. Such things promote controversial speculations rather than advancing God's work—which is by faith. (1 Timothy 1:3-4, NIV)

We see a possible slant in translation differences in verse 3. Some translations (e.g. NASB) say certain men, whereas the NIV says "certain people" and the NLT says "those whose teaching." The word in the original there is *tis*, an indefinite pronoun in the Greek, which means "people" is a more accurate rendering than "men." I believe that means that there may have been a concern that some women may have been teaching "myths and endless genealogies." That emphasis is repeated in chapter four. Consider what we read in verses 1-3 and 7.

> ¹The Spirit clearly says that in later times some will abandon the faith and follow deceiving spirits and things taught by demons. ²Such teachings come through hypocritical liars, whose consciences have been seared as with a hot iron. ³They forbid people to marry and order them to abstain from certain foods, which God created to be received with thanksgiving by those who believe and who know the truth…⁷Have nothing to do with godless myths and old wives' tales; rather, train yourself to be godly. (1 Timothy 4:1-3; 7, NIV)

At this time, Timothy was overseeing the church in Ephesus. When we examine what was taking place in the city, we can see the reasons for Paul's concern. At that time, Ephesus was the home of the world's largest and perhaps most expansive temple shrine, which was also considered one of the seven wonders of the ancient world. The temple was dedicated to the goddess Artemis (Diana), who was worshipped as a goddess of fertility, the nurturing progenitor, the one initiating life of the human race. The influence of the Artemis cult was extensive and when we read of the riot caused when Paul preached the worship of Jesus over Artemis in Acts 19, we begin to see how the cult was deeply ingrained in society. This created serious tension in the city between the long-standing following of Artemis and the new sect, often called "the Way." Many church historians say that the church in Ephesus ultimately became the largest Christian church in its day, numbering up to fifty thousand believers. With numbers of that magnitude, there were probably thousands of house churches under Timothy's apostolic leadership.

There is no doubt in my mind the believers in Ephesus were winning converts from the cult of Artemis into their church family. And since the cult was dedicated to the worship of the goddess, there would have been a preponderance of women under its influence. Many of these women would have come into the church with a warped, cult-influenced understanding of creation, thinking that the primary god was a woman and that woman was created first.

All of this ties in to what Paul is addressing in chapter 2, verses 11 and 12. He says that women should learn quietly and should not teach in any way that might bring harm to the body of believers. *Authenteō*, as it was used in Paul's day, wasn't simply demonstrating authority over someone; it had a subversive intent behind it. It has been shown in some instances to have a meaning of instigating harm, even bringing harm to one's self through suicide. Since the teachings of Artemis cult also had strong Gnostic beliefs, most notably that woman had precedence over man, Timothy's role as apostle was to see that no such teaching would undermine the true creation revelation. That may be why, in verse 13, he declares that Adam was created first. Not that being created first made him superior (if that were so creatures like fish and birds would be ranked above humans), but so that the revelation of creation as stated in Genesis was reliable.

I also find it notable that Paul is quick to say that Eve was deceived. It astonishes me when I hear preachers who blame the condition of our world and humanity on women, a spin-off of the myth of Pandora's box. If we read the temptation story carefully we find:

> When the woman saw that the fruit of the tree was good for food and pleasing to the eye, and also desirable for gaining wisdom, she took some and ate it. She also gave some to her husband, who was with her, and he ate it. (Genesis 3:6, NIV)

Adam was with Eve as this whole scenario unfolded. He had been charged with working the garden, taking care of it and guarding it. But when his helper was confronted by the serpent, he took no steps to interfere. He remained silent, neither engaging with his wife, nor challenging what she had been told. Adam had been told not to eat of the tree; he should have remembered the prohibition and spoken a reminder of that word into the situation. So, Paul rightly states both in Romans 5 and 1 Corinthians 15 that it was Adam's sin which changed human history and required the redemptive sacrifice of Jesus to rescue humanity from eternal separation from the Father.

There is also a literary device which Paul employed in this section called a chiasm. In a chiasm, a list of ideas or thoughts is structured in a way so that the first item parallels the last item, the second parallels the next to last and so on. For purposes of illustration, I'll use an example extracted from Duvall and Hayes'

Grasping God's Word (3rd edition, Zondervan, Grand Rapids, 2012), the Bible textbook which we used when we taught Bible interpretation at our school. From the following brief story we can see chiastic structure: I got up this morning, got dressed and drove to town. I worked hard all day, returned home, put on my pajamas and went to bed.

The parallels look like this:

    a I got up this morning
        b got dressed
            c and drove to town
                d I worked hard all day
            c^1 returned home
        b^1 put on my pajamas
    a^1 and went to bed.

Some chiasms have a central message, and some are simply parallelisms to add emphasis. When the middle point does not have a parallel, such as "I worked hard all day" in our example, it serves as the main point or idea in the chiasm. In his study of this passage in 1 Timothy 2, Perriman sees Eve as the central point of the chiasm in this passage, which he interprets to mean that Paul is really focusing on what went wrong in the garden of Eden. He shows the chiasm like this:

    a 11 Let a woman in quietness learn in all submission. . .
        b 13 For Adam was formed first,
            c then Eve,
        b' 14 and Adam was not deceived.
    a' But the woman, having been deceived, has come into transgression.

For Perriman, this passage is Paul's warning to women not to come under the influence of deceptive teaching and thus be prone to misleading others.

I will not pretend this is an easy passage to understand, but I draw on something that Kris Vallotton has said in his preaching on this matter, "I may not be able to tell you exactly what it does mean, but I can tell you what it does not mean." My conclusion is that this passage deals with a specific set of circumstances and is not a universal prohibition against women teaching, preaching or leading.

Lest you conclude this is too narrow a view of this verse, limiting it to a specific set of circumstances, let me show that this is not an unusual tactic for Paul. In fact, he does something very similar in Titus. Look at what Paul writes in Titus 1:10-11.

> *For there are many rebellious people, full of meaningless talk and deception, especially those of the circumcision group. They must be silenced, because they are disrupting whole households by teaching things they ought not to teach—and that for the sake of dishonest gain. (NIV)*

This particular group of individuals was maintaining that, according to Old Testament law, one could only become a believer after being circumcised. This was a long-standing problem against which Paul argued vehemently (see Galatians 1) and it was affecting Titus's congregations as well. Paul was addressing concerns specific to the people and settings of churches he knew about and was giving direction to stand against them. From both of these passages we can extract principles that may apply in our day. Apostles are called to affirm the truth of grace and to keep legalism, wherein God's acceptance can be earned, from taking root in the church. In all cases, they must guard against deceptive teachings that would lead the body of Christ away from true obedience to God's commands.

Although these passages address specific concerns that arose in that time and place, we can still extract principles from them which may apply in our day. For example, we should always approach the word of God with an attitude of submitting to its authority (verse 11). And we should also be aware of any anger and disagreement within our church bodies and work them through so our worship is not affected by dissension (verse 8).

1 TIMOTHY 3:1-12

*Here is a trustworthy saying: Whoever aspires to be an overseer desires a noble task. Now the overseer is to be above reproach, faithful to his wife, temperate, self-controlled, respectable, hospitable, able to teach, not given to drunkenness, not violent but gentle, not quarrelsome, not a lover of money. *^{4}*He must manage his own family well and see that his children obey him, and he must do so in a manner worthy of full respect. *^{5}*(If anyone does not know how to manage his own family, how can he take care of God's church?) He must not be a recent convert, or he may become conceited and fall under the same judgment as the devil. He must also have a good reputation with outsiders, so that he will not fall into disgrace and into the devil's trap.*

*In the same way, deacons are to be worthy of respect, sincere, not indulging in much wine, and not pursuing dishonest gain. *^{9}*They must keep hold of the deep truths of the faith with a clear conscience. *^{10}*They must first be tested; and then if there is nothing against them, let them serve as deacons.*

> *In the same way, the women are to be worthy of respect, not malicious talkers but temperate and trustworthy in everything.*
>
> *A deacon must be faithful to his wife and must manage his children and his household well. Those who have served well gain an excellent standing and great assurance in their faith in Christ Jesus.* (1 Timothy 3:1-12, NIV)

In the first letter Timothy received from Paul, Paul lists qualifications for church leaders. While many versions of the Bible translate the word *tis* in verse 1 to "man," the Greek word is actually an indefinite pronoun that should be read as "whoever" or "someone." 1 Timothy 3:1 then reads, "Whoever aspires to be an overseer desires a noble task." Paul then goes on to describe desirable attributes for men considered for leadership roles. I have mentioned the verb *proistēmi* before, but it bears repeating that "managing" in verse 4 is a "term which demands an effective exercise of authority bolstered by a character of integrity and sensitive compassion. Its use in verse 5 with the verb "take care of" defines the quality of leadership as related more to showing mercy than to delivering ultimatums."[9]

Here it seems easy to make an argument based on silence. Since Paul gives a lengthy list of qualifications for male leaders, we could infer that a failure to mention women perhaps implies that they should not hold leadership positions. While that is possible, I do not believe it to be the case. First, a clarification: according to the NIV, Paul suggests that men in this role should "be faithful" to their wives. The ESV says, "the husband of one wife." The literal translation is a "one-woman man." If we consider the culture of Paul's day, I believe he was warning that polygamists and men

---

9 Thomas Lea and Hayne P. Griffin. *1, 2 Timothy, Titus. The New American Commentary* (Vol. 34, p. 112). (Nashville, TN: Broadman & Holman Publishers, 1992).

who regularly had relations with multiple partners should not be considered for church leadership. Given the tendency for men to leave household management to their wives, Paul, by contrast, advocates for the active engagement and shared responsibility of men in the home.

As the letter continues, Paul speaks about the office of deacon (servant leadership at its best). In verses 8 to 10, several translations limit the role to men. Consider the NASB:

> *Deacons likewise must be men of dignity, not double-tongued, or addicted to much wine or fond of sordid gain, but holding to the mystery of the faith with a clear conscience. These men must also first be tested; then let them serve as deacons if they are beyond reproach. (1 Timothy 3:8-10, NASB)*

The word "men" does not show up in the original text, in either verse 8 or verse 10, so we are witnessing a bias for exclusively male leadership from the translators. I believe the new NIV (2011), quoted above, is a much more accurate representation of the Greek text.

Verse 11 is dealt with differently depending on the translation. It begins with the phrase "in the same way," which I believe means Paul has switched to address qualifications for women leaders. The list of qualifications for women is shorter than the list for men, however women dealt with fewer cultural issues that required Paul's reproach. Women were monogamous and accustomed to managing their households. Some take issue with the word *gunaikas*, sometimes translated as "wives," assuming that Paul could only be speaking of the wives of the male leaders in question (see NLT, ESV and KJV). Kittel is quite clear that while this word can mean wife, it most often refers to a woman of marriageable age. "In general Greek from the time of Homer, as also in the LXX (Septuagint, the Greek translation of the Old Testament) and the New Testament, *gunā* denotes the "female" as distinct from the male."[10] I believe Paul mentions women because he knew of so many who held positions of responsibility in the churches he founded, and he highly valued the feminine voice in the leadership process. As I said earlier, as a family benefits from having influence from both parents in the lives of their children, so the church benefits when the female perspective is sought, honored and united with its male counterpart.

---

10 Geoffrey W. Bromiley. *Theological Dictionary of the New Testament*. (Grand Rapids, MI: Eerdmans, 1985).

Sixth Chapter

PARTNERING TOGETHER

From the earliest days of human history, God envisioned men and women working together: "let us make them in our image and let them rule." Obviously, the enemy of our souls saw the power of bringing separation and exclusion into that joint stewardship. When we hear the blame-shifting in the first few pages of Scripture ("the woman that you gave me", "the serpent deceived me"), we realize nothing has really changed. The prevalence of accusation and finger pointing in our culture today should call us to look again at God's original intention and seek His solutions. Jesus came to destroy the works of the devil (1 John 3:8) and to undo the effects of the curse (Galatians 3:13). We can see that there are mindsets that require adjustment for men and women to work and relate effectively together, whether at home, in the church, in the workplace or in society.

In His wisdom, God replaces the old with the new, bringing wholeness instead of brokenness. We see this theme in Isaiah 61:

> *The Spirit of the Sovereign Lord is on me, because the Lord has anointed me to proclaim good news to the poor...and provide for those who grieve in Zion— to bestow on them a crown of beauty instead of ashes, the oil of joy instead of mourning, and a garment of praise instead of a spirit of despair. They will be called oaks of righteousness, a planting of the Lord for the display of his splendor. (Isaiah 61:1;3, NIV)*

When God sees harmful attributes showing up in our lives, he offers us an opportunity to exchange what we have for something better, provisions often reflecting the opposite of what we have been experiencing: beauty, joy and praise, instead of depression, mourning and despair. He does the "instead of" work within us; then it is our responsibility to bring about changes in our thoughts and actions. Paul has some suggestions for correcting judgmental mindsets in 2 Corinthians.

> *The weapons we fight with are not the weapons of the world. On the contrary, they have divine power to demolish strongholds. We demolish arguments and every pretension that sets itself up against the knowledge of God, and we take captive every thought to make it obedient to Christ. And we will be ready to punish every act of disobedience, once your obedience is complete. You are judging by appearances. If anyone is confident that they belong to Christ, they should consider again that we belong to Christ just as much as they do. (2 Corinthians 10:4-7, NIV)*

While that language may sound strong, I assure you that underneath many of our misconceptions and misunderstandings regarding the importance of women's voice and roles are long-standing lies of the enemy which need to be demolished. We have faulty estimations of one another. I think that the King James captures the idea when it calls them vain imaginations. Too often, our egos mix into our judgments, causing them to focus on negative criticism of others. We have judged others based simply on external observations, physical appearance, for example, instead of understanding their hearts.

In the Christian walk, we need to have our minds renewed and be trained in righteousness to undo our long-standing negative attitudes and prejudices. In particular, where we have maintained a hierarchical, "top down" understanding of church leadership, we must work to apply what Jesus taught us in Matthew.

> *Jesus called them together and said, "You know that the rulers of the Gentiles lord it over them, and their high officials exercise authority over them. Not so with you. Instead, whoever wants to become great among you must be your servant, and whoever wants to be first must be your slave—just as the Son of Man did not come to be served, but to serve, and to give his life as a ransom for many." (Matthew 20:25-28, NIV)*

Jesus says that we should not make it our aim to lord over others, but to serve them as he did, motivated by an attitude of love.

As we move toward submission to one another, we realize that neither men nor women are the enemy. We have only one true enemy and, as we saw in Genesis 3:15, his deep enmity burns toward women. This has caused centuries of female oppression and exclusion from influence. I do not believe we are all the same; we have different gifts according to the grace given to us (Romans 12:6). However, our gifts are not "gender exclusive." Men and women may fulfill different roles depending on their gifts and calling.

Healthy partnership requires understanding as Peter defines it in 1 Peter.

> *Likewise, husbands, live with your wives in an understanding way, showing honor to the woman as the weaker vessel, since they are heirs with you of the grace of life, so that your prayers may not be hindered.* (1 Peter 3:7, ESV)

We can and should value the unique perspective that comes from the feminine understanding. "The purposes of a person's heart are deep waters, but one who has understanding draws them out," we are told in Proverbs 20:5. We need to take the initiative to draw them out and then realize we can "stand under" their thoughts.

There are "general" gender traits unique to both men and women, however each of us has a unique blend of both, which does not compromise our male or female core. Cooking or doing housework doesn't make you less of a man any more than enjoying rugby or hunting make you less of a woman. We can adjust to one another without ceasing to be who we really are. Ephesians 4:16 says that He makes the whole body fit together perfectly. As each part does its own special work, it helps the other parts grow, so that the whole body is healthy, growing and full of love. Please note who helps this happen.

We should recognize men and women can have different tendencies. Men tend to be task-oriented and women tend to be relationship oriented, yet, women are very competent in accomplishing tasks and men are very capable of meaningful relationships. In healthy partnerships, teams are built and tasks are completed successfully. With regard to problem solving, women often socialize and men often internalize. Women tend to move in collaboration and cooperation in order to reach wise solutions. We see this in Scripture as women gather at the cross and then travel to the empty tomb, prepared to embalm Jesus' body. When men want to focus on a problem, they will often isolate such as when Elijah ran off to his cave, or they may retreat to a familiar diversion as when Peter went back to fishing, to have some time to process. All of this recognizes that we are different; coming together makes for a synergy where the sum of the parts creates a greater whole.

Some final thoughts as we close. Jesus is calling His church to move away from being a divided house in order to become a united army, focused on destroying the works of the devil and bringing people to wholeness through complete salvation. Together, as co-laboring men and women, we represent the complete picture of God's heart. Often, the case will arise where the best leader for a situation will be a woman who exhibits the necessary gifts and talents for the job - not because a man is unavailable, but because she represents God's best first choice.

In closing, consider this final Scripture from the Message Bible:

> *May our dependably steady and warmly personal God develop maturity in you so that you get along with each other as well as Jesus gets along with us all. Then we'll be a choir—not our voices only, but our very lives singing in harmony in a stunning anthem to the God and Father of our Master Jesus! So reach out and welcome one another to God's glory. Jesus did it; now you do it! (Romans 15:5-7)*

THE OTHER HALF OF THE ARMY

Seventh Chapter

SOME PERSONAL ACCOUNTS

As I noted in the preface, I interviewed four women in various positions of ministry and church leadership to offer personal testimonies alongside the biblical justification that God's heart intends the full participation of women in His Kingdom. Their stories are included to give you some idea of the various obstacles woman face today when they respond to a call to ministry and how, through God's help, they overcome adversity.

SHERI HESS

Sheri Hess pastors alongside her husband, David, at Christ Community Church in Camp Hill, PA. She is a motivator, engaging people with her transparent style of communication. Encouragement and enthusiasm pour out of her life. As a teacher and compassionate voice to this generation, her greatest desire is to see people step into their God-given destiny. Sheri and Dave have three adult children and three precious grandchildren.

Can women have authority in the church? That's where the rub is. For me, [the call to ministry] was a thing that just evolved. When I was younger, because of my personality, I was always put in leadership roles; it's just the way I'm woven and wired. I knew I was supposed to be a leader; I just felt validated in those areas. By the time I went to Messiah College, I knew I wanted to serve God. I double majored in Christian Education and Behavioral Science because I love people. When I met [my husband] Dave freshman year, I was interpreting that my call was to be his wife, to be a partner with him. And yet, there was this nagging thing inside of me that thought *there's more that I want to use you for.* I felt this authority and I knew I had it, but there were very few role models for me of women in positions of leadership in the church. On one hand, there were very liberal people: my dad's sister was a radical feminist. One of her friends was a lawyer who was actually contracted to help work on the committee to take maleness out of the Bible. All the male references to Jesus and God as the Father or Jesus as Son were taken out and made either feminine or bisexual. I knew that wasn't right. So, we ended up connecting with people from a fellowship of churches opposed to women in leadership roles, because we met them at the Jesus Rally. They were thinking of advocating to put the covering back on women because they had a particular view of submission. I was there and thought that wasn't right either. So, I had a steady diet of that's not right, but I didn't see an alternative where I would fit in.

When I became a pastor, I found that most people who came against my decision to pastor weren't men. Most of my opposition has come from women, which was really hard for me. I didn't understand it other than culturally. I've learned that women and men have different cultures. In female culture, you must be sweet. You must not stand out; you must blend in. In male culture, you're allowed to boast, you're allowed to be an individual. Both cultures affect the way we lead. I did a whole teaching for the Beautiful One conference a couple years ago on the differences between the ways in which ladies and men lead. I've learned that, when I lead meetings with all women, we always have connection time, sometimes talking 70% of our time on personal issues and accomplishing everything else in record time because we connected at a heart level first instead of deliberating. That's because female culture is feeling-oriented, intuitive and relational. In women's culture, when we're talking, we're doing active listening, giving each other non-verbal clues, like making eye contact and responding with aha, ohh and mmhmm. Guys are often frustrated watching that - they prefer things be said succinctly, straight up with relatively no emotion. When I'm in male-dominated meetings, I'm learning to swing with that style.

As far as pursuing leadership goes, I remember sharing with a female Global student one time that a lot of churches are looking at their long-held views of roles women can play. I reminded her that if you are raised up to work alongside men, please remember we're not trying to be raised up to take over. God is interested in making great partnerships in this hour. Sometimes, if you want to make an impact, you're going to have to play by the rules that are currently there so that we can work alongside men. She responded that this approach wasn't very fair. "Why do we have to be the ones to change?" she asked. I explained that it's a choice to honor. Hopefully in ten years the cultural differences between men and women will have been refined and we'll work better together as men and women, but for now, we're trying to mobilize the other half of the army.

Years ago, I read a book by a communication specialist by the name of Deborah Tannen. That book was life for me. I was able to take and modify her material to develop five areas of adjustment for women to have an impact when working with men. One, when meeting with guys, skip the details, get straight to the point, the bottom line. Second, if there are too many details you lose them. In our world, women talk for relationship, men talk for knowledge. I have learned in meeting with guys to assume that they have heard me the first time I share information and not keep repeating myself. Three, I have learned in meeting with guys not to try to connect with them in ways that do not bring life. Women connect by talking about their troubles, but guys don't understand this form of bonding. They see themselves as problem solvers. Four, I have learned to change my communication style knowing that fruit will come from the adjustment. And five, ultimately, it's about honor, which is another word for love. To me, shifting my culture when working with men is loving them enough to communicate the way they need it.

Fighting through years of resistance to women in ministry has been really difficult, even painful at times. It feels hard for me not to take it personally; it's hard not to fight it. You sense every liberty in the Gospel, but you don't have any freedom. What has brought me comfort is the role of the Holy Spirit as the advocate, making a way for me where there was no way. The Holy Spirit, I think, has been my biggest advocate, just whispering to me, "Come on, you've got this." I'm just praying that my daughters don't have to go through that same struggle.

What it comes down to, in this season, is that God is trying to build his church. In that, we can't forget women's culture or communication style preferences. I believe He's calling us to a place of more intimacy for revival, more than we've ever had before. Even when we don't know what's ahead, God is trying to help us connect at a deeper level. As we go deeper, we need to be able to access, and be comfortable with, women's style. It's not just about having good information, we need the emotion, sensitivity and intuition to connect at a deeper level. How many people would feel a sense of inclusion, camaraderie, belonging and acceptance if we learned to marry the two styles?

Both men and women are made in His image. I used to believe that just the guys were the image, but in Genesis 1:28, when He wanted to paint a picture to say "This is what I look like", He made male and female. He made THEM in His image, together. They are a complete representation of who he is together. If we have an all-male leadership or even all-female leadership I think it distorts the image of God. However, if you have men and women partnering together, that is a complete picture of who He is. Then, we can RE-present Him to the world.

DR. KIM MAAS

Dr. Kim Maas is an ordained Foursquare Pastor. She is a gifted directional leader, prophetic preacher, pastor and mentor, as well as devoted wife, mother, and grandmother. Her passion is to inspire, encourage and equip God's people to move forward toward fulfilling the call of God on their lives. This passion comes through in her preaching, leadership, writing, and everyday life.

I was called to ministry on March 22, 1994, basically at the same time that I received the baptism of the Holy Spirit. I was attending a 4-square church, but it was a very seeker-sensitive church. I really had no idea that it was any different than my Baptist upbringing. The reason I was in a church at that point was because God had saved my marriage miraculously: I heard the audible voice of God during a time when my husband and I were divorcing. So, I felt like I owed a lot to God. I had been invited to a women's retreat for the first time in my life for the weekend of March 22, and I was asked to give my testimony regarding that miraculous event in my life. Afterwards, a young woman approached me and asked if she could lay hands on me to impart the baptism of the Holy Spirit. I had heard about impartation before, but I wasn't sure if it was real. In my upbringing, because I had grown up in a cessationist Baptist church, I had heard that those things were not from the Lord. There are charismatic Baptist churches in this day and age, but the one that I went to was cessationist in its doctrine. However, I was willing to let her pray, so she laid hands on me and, of course, I had a radical encounter with the Holy Spirit. I sort of went into this other place; I don't remember seeing or hearing anything. I just know that there were moments when I was out of touch. The next thing I know, I'm sitting in a chair, and I'm crying. I feel something in my body that I've never felt before. I didn't immediately start speaking in tongues or anything like that—that happened the next day—but I started hearing from the Lord like in a stream. It was the same voice I had heard audibly, although this time it came from inside of me. I heard a voice and saw a vision of a garden. Pests had come into the garden, but I also saw how water and sunshine were coming into the garden. The Lord said, "I'm going to call you to the garden, which is my people, and you're going to water my garden." It was in that moment that I knew the interpretation of that vision meant full-time vocational ministry. Don't ask me how I put that together, but I just know that's absolutely what the vision was about.

I knew the vision was from the Lord. During a time of communion the church leaders suggested we ask the Lord if he wanted to say anything to us. That was new to me, but I heard the Lord call me to full-time ministry. Immediately, I found myself facing a number of questions. What does that even look like? What does that mean for me? What does that mean for my family, for our hopes and dreams? The other challenge, probably the greater challenge, was if it was even possible.

In my context growing up, women weren't ministers. We could work in children's ministry, we could bring food to the potluck on Sunday…all of that was women's work: to teach the kids and to bring the food. I thought that's what we were supposed to be doing. It seemed like every women's ministry event I went to, even in the church I was a part of before I received the call focused on the best way to clean house and how to be a good mom. And 'how to be a good mom' meant if you were a Christian mother, you were a stay-at-home mom who also homeschooled your children. I was a full time RN working in pediatrics and labor and delivery, and I was always made to feel guilty because I had a career outside my home.

I received the call to full-time ministry and I just told the Lord, I don't know where to start with all this, but I'll serve wherever you open a door to me. That's how it all began. Of course, I started in children's ministry. I love children, but as far as ministry goes when the Holy Spirit comes, I'm probably not very kid-friendly. After that, I was asked to do women's ministry, which I did faithfully, but I didn't love it. I love women, I just don't like traditional women's ministry. Pretty soon, doors kept opening in the church where I was serving. I was asked to be on the church council and then I was asked to be on their leadership team in other ways, and I became a prayer leader for the church. I worked with the youth, probably like most people who are coming up through the ranks. But I worried a lot about being a woman, even as I started to be given small moments on a platform in front of God's people. It was so ingrained in me from my upbringing that women shouldn't do that.

Around the same time, I started having encounters with the Holy Spirit: visions, dreams and impressions. Suddenly, I would just know something. I was hearing His voice in my church, but we didn't really have any teaching about such things. I didn't know where to go, but I had heard that a lot of this was going on at Harvest Rock Church in Pasadena. So I started driving to conferences at Harvest Rock just so I could be around people who were having this stuff happen to them and talking about it.

Within a year from the original call at that first retreat, I had a major vision. That was the first time God actually showed me what He was going to send me out to do. I knew that I was going to be in leadership. I knew that I was going to be ministering to God's people, which meant men and women, and I knew it involved opening my mouth because He showed me a platform and a microphone. At that point, God started speaking to me about preaching and speaking and prophesying all over the world

In 2002, the Lord spoke to me and asked me to go to seminary. Honestly, I had to look up the word seminary because I didn't know what it meant. On the very first day of seminary while driving to my first class, I was listening to the radio in my car and I heard the voice of a prominent West Coast pastor stating that women in church leadership was a doctrine of demons. I started sobbing. It was just devastating. I thought to myself, Here I am Lord, on my way to train for full-time vocational ministry to preach and speak and prophecy around the world and it's a doctrine of demons?! I didn't know how to reconcile that because I really believed what he said.

When I got to school that day, I went into the office and asked to talk to someone. I had an advisor, a man named Dr. David Dorman, who was an amazing man. He was Presbyterian, charismatic and very understanding. He sat down with me, and he talked me through all the different positions on women's role in ministry. He said, "I can tell you about this Kim but, you're going to have to decide…You're going to have to take a stand theologically on your own because you're the one called to your ministry." I spent a semester learning about all the various positions of women in leadership. Since then, I think I've become very "egalitarian." I just think we're all made in the image of God: we're all equal in everything and we submit to one another equally.

It was quite a struggle for me because I had to really think through the issue and undo the theology that I'd been taught. I honored my upbringing, but I was mad at those responsible for the wrong messages I received and believed. I knew in order for me to go forward, the first thing I had to settle was my heart and mind. I had to settle biblically and theologically that I could be a leader in the church. Right after that I started getting into some real leadership in the church. I became licensed as a pastor. I helped plant a church. I became the senior executive leader at a little church here in my hometown where I remained in that capacity until two years ago when I went itinerant.

The responses I received as a woman in ministry were varied. We had people in the church sending us letters explaining they were leaving because they didn't believe in women in ministry. And we had people walk out of the service because I stood up and went to the platform to preach. Many times I have heard, "That's really good preaching for a woman." (What's that supposed to mean?) Even in my own denominational context, there have been times when I've been invited to higher level leadership meetings and have walked into the room with my husband, who would be greeted as Pastor Maas, assuming that Pastor Maas had to be a man. Please hear me, I am not offended by any of this. But, even though we're in the 21st century, I have faced all these things, and I think most women do.

The interesting thing is, I experienced this not just from men but also from women. I have actually had women say to me, "I don't know if I could be comfortable with a woman senior pastor. I just feel like senior pastors should be men." It's always interesting to hear. Why is that? I really believe it's because that doctrine has been around for so long. There are times when this struggle deeply challenges me, and when that happens I try very hard not to keep it inside because that's when it will fester. I've learned that it's best to talk about it, write about it and pray about it. That's how I deal with the emotions. Very honestly, at this point I don't get affected much by it. There was something about God having me face all of this in seminary at the very beginning of my ministry, when I heard that horrible thing on the radio. I think going through that experience made me ready to face anything.

But some instances are harder to shake than others. For example, several years ago, I had a strong disagreement with a fellow pastor/leader in a church where I was serving. In cases of disagreement, and because I'm a woman, it's common that the word "Jezebel" gets thrown around. I'm a strong leader and I am very articulate about what I feel and think, so I deal with conflict by talking about it. But it's really unfair to be called a Jezebel in any way, shape, or form, simply because you have a strong personality and because you're female. Disagreeing strongly doesn't make you a Jezebel. I don't get affected much by these issues any longer, but the Jezebel accusation took me a while to work through. I really had to go to the Lord. One of the things that I had to do was to ask the Lord, are these accusations true? I had to work through whether they were true or not. In the process, I learned the more transparent you can be with anything before the Lord and before others who really know you, the better off you'll be.

Despite all this, during my time in ministry, my strongest advocates have been men. For example, the senior leader that I was senior executive pastor with, who made that choice all those years ago, his name is Reggie Mercado. When he was considering who to bring on as a senior associate leader, I was the only woman among the candidates. He chose me based on qualifications, not at all on gender. That was a wonderful thing; we worked so well together and he was quite a champion for me. He really gave me complete and total freedom in the church to preach and teach and prophesy. I did all of the leadership development and I did a lot of mentoring of leaders and emerging leaders, and training; gender was never an issue. He just saw my gifting, knew I was supposed to be in leadership and that was it. When I was in seminary, my seminary was the Kings Seminary in Van Nuys, Jack Hayford's school. Most of my professors that really poured into me there were men. They really felt that I had an academic potential that needed to be called out and pursued, and that was amazing. And then, of course, since I met Randy Clark, he has become my spiritual father. I never had one before, honestly. He's the first and only spiritual father that I have, and that has been a very, very, special relationship. Dr. Allen Hawkins, Dr. Nick Goth, Dr. Rodney Hogue, Randy Clark, and Tom Jones - these 5 men have opened doors for me and poured into me. They make way for me, make room for me.

As we make more room for women in ministry, we see amazing things happen. In the church where I was the senior associate pastor, we noticed that our church drew some of the strongest women leaders in the marketplace who are churched, because I was there. Not because of me specifically, but because a strong woman leader was allowed to be in that place and regularly share on the platform. My voice was regularly heard there, and it was very obvious that we held both genders equally. We had such a large crop for a small church of very strong women. For example, there was one woman who was a lawyer who came to me one time after church, and she said, "I just have to tell you, I am so grateful every time I come here to see you up there, preaching and bringing prophetic words and leading the worship. It's so refreshing to me, because many years ago I felt called to leadership in the church. I couldn't find a place anywhere to serve except in children's ministry, so I went outside the church and became a lawyer."

I received comments like that a lot from women leaders in the market place. Because they weren't allowed to use their gifts inside the church, and because they never saw a model of women at a church, they never knew they were welcome to come and use their gifts in the church. In our little church, in this little town, because this senior pastor dared give me this position and such freedom, women were flocking in. My point is that's going to happen if we start opening up positions to women in our churches, ministries and organizations: amazingly gifted, strong women are going to start flocking in and they're going to start to use their gifts inside and outside of the church.

AARON HORTON

Aaron is the founding Pastor for Seek Church NYC and the director of Global Celebration School of Supernatural Ministry school in Manhattan. An anointed preacher, worship leader, songwriter, marketplace consultant and conference speaker, she has ministered throughout the United States and in thirty nations around the globe. Her ministry style is prophetic, joyful, and intimate with an extreme passion for the Presence of God. Aaron's life is dedicated to seeing God's Kingdom manifested on earth as it is in heaven as His love and power invade and change everything.

I grew up in a ministry family in Texas as a pastor's kid, missionary kid, and a kid involved in every aspect of local church. The fact that I "had no testimony" was distressing in my younger years, but as I got older I realized the absolute grace it was to be raised in the church. I asked Jesus in my heart at every meal prayer starting around age 6, and from there my deep love for God grew. As a teen, I led worship and went on missions trips with my youth group, but had no desire to have a career in traditional ministry. My desire to go into the secular music industry grew and I desired to be a "light in the darkness."

While studying theatre and fine art at the University of Texas, I attended a songwriting class at Christ for the Nations Bible School. That class instigated my love for leading worship, songwriting, and recording. In the early 90's, I did not know of many female worship leaders and the world of ministry seemed to be male-dominated.

I had no desire to preach, but was asked to teach vocal classes at worship conferences. Once I overcame the terror of teaching for the first time, I fell in love; something ignited in me. I had not pursued ministry, but was doing it nonetheless. I traveled all over the world with Christ for the Nations ministering, recording live worship albums, and leading worship conferences.

I was first rejected because of my gender during my involvement with a church plant leadership team. Despite my involvement on the leadership team, I found out later they didn't actually believe in women in ministry. They considered my leadership position to be "legal," because I was only singing. I remember meeting with the Pastor saying, "I need some clarity here. You're telling me that I can stand up in front of your congregation and can sing the Word, but I can't preach the Word? And I can preach to the children, or minister in another country as a missionary, but not here at home?" That was my first taste of the ridiculousness of women persecuted in ministry. At that time, I had no desire to preach, but the idea that I couldn't preach because of being female was absurd to me. Needless to say, my days at that church were very few.

Shortly after this encounter, I left the Dallas/Ft. Worth area and struck out on my own in Nashville, TN with a plan to pursue a career in the music industry. God opened up an opportunity to work and lead worship at a home for troubled teenagers and unwed mothers. That's where I really began falling in love with humans. Working at a home where girls' testimonies were far worse than any story I'd ever heard or could have imagined unlocked compassion in me. I will be forever grateful and honored for that season and the opportunity I was given to love beyond my ability to relate. Over the next few years in TN and NJ, I served in various local church ministries as a Creative Arts Director, Youth Pastor, Worship Leader, and Pastoral Executive Assistant.

In 2007, I was driving down a country road in Tennessee when out of my mouth came the question, "God, what do you want me to do?" I really could have gone anywhere and led worship because of my musical résumé, but nothing inside of me wanted to be a part of another church. The response I heard shocked me. God responded, "What do YOU want to do?" In that moment, God began to open my eyes to see something I could have never imagined.

I scheduled an appointment to tell my pastor that I was going to leave Nashville and move to New York City. As I began to speak, the words came out of my mouth, "I am moving to NY to raise up a ministry and training center for men and women who are going to take the King and Kingdom into every sphere of influence inside and outside the four walls of church." The more I talked, the more excited I became. I had never heard of anything like what I was describing. The concept was completely foreign to me, and I remember leaving the meeting thinking, "That sounds like the best idea ever!"

In December, a few days before Christmas, I moved to NYC with a friend. We had neither ministry contacts nor money, but had amazing family members and incredible mentors and pastors cheering us on from a distance in our pioneering adventure with God. It was so encouraging to know they were excited to see what God was doing with us in the city and were committed to spiritually covering us.

New York was the first time I wasn't serving someone else's vision, or under someone else's ministry. It was a little unnerving in the beginning because neither the ministry, nor I, seemed to fit in any easily explainable category. But we began having nights of worship in our empty apartment and people came. They invited friends and God birthed Creative Kingdom Expression right there in my living room. Years later, over a thousand people have come through that room.

God is funny in the way He never gives me much warning about big changes in my life. He knows I am likely to overanalyze the details and freak out in moments that require leaps of faith. Not long after I moved to NYC, God began to thrust me into conference arenas to lead worship and to speak. I remember attending a meeting with a wild Bulgarian named Georgian Banov. I remember going up for prayer with one of my team members and before I knew it Georgian had pulled us up on stage saying, "These two mighty women of God are evangelists to New York City and will be leading my afternoon session on Wednesday. They're going to prophesy and give words of knowledge to everyone in the room." At that time, I could not have imagined Georgian would later become my spiritual father, or that I would end up becoming the director of his supernatural school in NYC.

When Wednesday came, I remember thinking, "I've never released words of knowledge or prophesied over an entire room!" So, I did what any responsible leader would do and called a few of my friends and told them I needed their help praying for people Wednesday afternoon. I didn't tell them exactly what we were going to do, because they probably wouldn't have come. That afternoon, eight of us did what we had never done before. From our courageous "yes," we experienced the Presence of God crashing in the room. Those in attendance were touched and my team and I were never the same.

I am a single female in full-time ministry in Manhattan. I lead Creative Kingdom Expression and have founded Seek Church NYC, which is now in its third year. We did not open to the public for the first two years, as God had me sow into my leadership team for that season as He secured our foundation. There is honestly nothing like this beautiful church in the city. I stay overwhelmed by God's love for this treasure!

When God told me to start this church, I thought, "Seriously, You're going to put a bigger target on my back? Not only am I a female in ministry, but you want me to pastor a church as a single woman in New York City? Really?" But honestly, I have been nothing but blessed. I have not experienced pushback as a female except a few times.

My heart's desire is to be married, and while there are moments when I feel alone, I have watched God be my brilliant defender, my safe place, and my confidence. He is my partner and my deepest love. He is the Man in my life and has surrounded me with amazing male and female leaders. I know there are some who have said, "Men will never go to Pastor Aaron's church," but I just laugh when I hear stuff like that. I recognize this is God's deal. It's not up to me. I'm going to be here even if it's just me. I'm going to follow what He's doing no matter our gender ratio.

One of the things I knew I didn't want was a ministry with all women. I had no point to prove. I just see humans with distinct characteristics of God. He gives us the strategy to create safe places for women and men alike to rise up in their identity as sons and daughters first, then as ministers. One of my deepest passions is pulling greatness out of the ones around me. So whether traveling for ministry or in my church or school, it is a privilege to share the stage and let them shine. It's a beautiful thing to see men and women alike, stepping up as leaders at Seek Church, knowing they probably wouldn't be given that opportunity this early on in many places. Each time they speak, they blow my mind. I am blown away to be doing life with my heroes. My friends and leaders are some of the strongest men and women I've ever met in ministry. They are co-laboring with God and with one another. Never once has there been a male/female issue. Never once has there been a power struggle on either side. No one needs to defend themselves because of who they are or their gender. We are honored to empower women and men at the same time!

We do this by creating an atmosphere for men and women alike to be great. We're not going to let anyone sit on the sidelines and hide. It's been really beautiful to see women who have never really been empowered come to our church and taste freedom. But what's so cool is that the men experience the exact same thing. It's awesome when I hear that from the women, but when it's from the guys, my heart is really glad.

My story is a little different from other women who have struggled through ministry. By God's grace, I can't tell you the last time I actually felt fear or stress. That isn't because I am anything special; I am just a daughter of God. He told me that I was created to receive His love, and so I focus on being the best receiver of His love. Even if that means I don't ever minister again, I know my life is pleasing to Him. I don't have anything to prove as a woman, a minister, a single, or even as a human. So, I choose to live in this win-win situation and that takes the pressure off of my performance. I'm here as a recipient of God's love, period. Everything else is icing on the cake and becomes an outflow of that reality.

CARLA PRATICO

Outside of being a Pastor of Seek Church, Carla runs a successful branding and marketing company, Polus Digital, Inc, as well as a life consulting firm. Her businesses are truly a partnership with God in every way. She pursues His presence throughout her workday, asking God for guidance, and holding her work to a standard of Kingdom excellence. Carla has a desire to see Christians do business and life differently than the world and experience the abundant blessings for which Jesus paid such a high price. She loves to help believers get free from busyness as they run their businesses and also unlocked into their purpose so they can live fully alive to God while expanding the Kingdom here on earth.

I got pretty radically saved in a Manhattan bar on my 23rd birthday and a month later was filled with the Holy Spirit. Since that day, the idea of my life being a co-laboring ministry with Jesus was so clear to me. I had this understanding that with the power of the Holy Spirit living in me, I was equipped to do the work, to heal the sick, cast out demons, and cleanse the lepers, so I did. I started praying for people on the street and seeing really unbelievable miracles happen almost right away.

The back story is that I grew up going sporadically to a very conservative church. It didn't feel like there was any power there, and that's what my heart desired even at a young age. I needed to know there was a God who could heal and do the miraculous. I needed to know there was a God who was interested in my life and in me. As far as I could tell, that wasn't true. When I was told God wasn't actually powerful, He became to me a God that didn't seem worthy of my time or attention. But things changed after I got filled with the Holy Spirit. So many people I prayed for were getting healed. People were getting out of wheelchairs, torn ACLs were fixed without surgery, and legs were growing out and back pain was being healed for good. In that season, the God that I had always hoped was real, was making Himself known to me in such a powerful way that ministry became such an enjoyable and natural part of my life.

Shortly after being saved, I started going to Pastor Aaron Horton's house meetings and really saw her as a powerful and groundbreaking woman in ministry. She wasn't running a church at the time, but she was just opening her home for people to encounter the love of God. Those nights on her living room floor impacted me so deeply. I learned how to love myself and that God's purpose in creating me was first and foremost simply to love me. So, I just started showing up whenever Aaron had a meeting or gathering because I knew her message was so powerful and important for the body of Christ to hear. And thankfully, she's the type of person who will push you into the deep end before you're ready to swim. She started asking me to minister with her when I had only been saved about a year!

When Georgian Banov invited Aaron and her NYC team of ministers to come and prophesy at a conference, I had never really prophesied before. And yet, I found myself standing in front of a room of 200-300 people being told, "You can prophesy and hear from God, so go for it." I remember thinking, "Lord, I trust that I hear from you." That experience of being trusted with hearing from the Lord for all those people helped me grow and gave me so much confidence in my ability to hear from God.

Within the next few years, I really started pastoring when Aaron opened her church and asked my husband and me to be senior pastors. I've been teaching, ministering, and pastoring on a larger scale ever since. I got saved in 2010 and we came on the Seek Church team in 2014.

We haven't experienced nearly as much pushback in the ministry as we expected. There's something about the liberal environment of NYC that has broken through some of that. I think it's because women have made such progress in the business world that it only makes sense that that would be reflected in ministry as well. I've never met another female senior pastor or church planter, so it certainly can feel like we are pioneering new territory here. Still, I've not experienced too much pushback. The thing that I have noticed the most that has been pretty disappointing is seeing conference lineups where the only woman on the lineup is a worship leader. That is a pretty consistent occurrence, to see only men lead and teach at conferences. You know, there are the exceptions of Heidi

Baker and Patricia King, but even at smaller-level conferences it ends up being either a women's conference with all female speakers or a conference where it's all male leaders. So, that's the one area that I've noticed where there hasn't been a ton of breakthrough for women. I think that some men aren't necessarily aware that we women need their advocacy. There are times when I wonder how organizers can't find one woman to be a guest speaker. I'm sure it's not intentional, but even that in itself - the lack of championing women - is concerning. It seems as though no one is standing up to affirm that we need to have a full representation of God's creation in the church for this to be a complete story.

On the other hand, we do have great support by a select group of men. Pastor Alan Smith of Catch the Fire in Dallas/Fort Worth area and Georgian Banov have been amazing cheerleaders for women in ministry. They have believed in our message and what we're doing in New York City. Also, just watching and learning about Heidi Baker has influenced me personally, as well. My whole life I searched for a role model. Before I was saved, I looked to all sorts of inspiring women but never really connected to them. Then when I got saved and I heard Heidi for the first time, it was as though my heart came alive to this woman who looked like what I had always dreamed of becoming. I knew then, if she can do it, I can do it.

Epilogue

I have been asked why I titled my book The Other Half of the Army. The phrase came to me when I thought about what the world would look like today if we hadn't strayed from God's original design when He said, "Let us make human beings in our image, to be like us. They will reign…" (Gen. 1:26, NLT). I imagined the world filled with the shalom of God and considered the conflict that could have been avoided had we never left the garden. Unfortunately, the fall plunged humanity into a war that separated mankind from its maker and invited division into human relationships, particularly those between men and women. Jesus came to reconcile humanity to the Godhead and to restore human relationships so that we might unite as an army and join him in the battle to win many to Christ. God's intent was, and I believe still is, for men and women to fight together in this battle, as one army. That is especially relevant as we confront all the darkness and evil in our world today.

Men and women have very different gifts, talents and perspectives, and we should celebrate these differences as we learn how they complement each other. Since God's design for all culture and society is family (growing out of the primary relationship of marriage), it makes sense that the basic building block of God's Kingdom, the church, would also depend on both male and female leadership.

When I discovered all the obstacles that have kept women from fully participating in the army of God, from patriarchal cultures to male-dominated traditions, to misogynistic viewpoints, I realized more than ever that my discomfort was valid and needed to be put to rest. As I interviewed women whose leadership I respect, I wondered why we have been content for so long with mostly male perspectives at the helm of church leadership. So I call on like-minded men to join me in becoming champions of women and to support them in every way as they answer the call of God in their lives.

This project has been an important journey for me. I remain committed more than ever to seeing women standing alongside men, ministering the full message of the Gospel and bringing heaven to earth. Whenever opportunities arise, I now pray and declare freedom over women, breaking off the power of negative, limiting words spoken over them, freeing them to be all that God is calling them to be. My challenge to the people of God is first to actively engage in meaningful dialog, women sharing their struggles and men coming to terms with the damage their influence and words have brought. We need to shift our paradigms, admit where we have made errors, then seek and offer forgiveness as needed, so more of the army can be fighting from an equal standing.

Epilogue

When the full army is on board we see both God's intended design and humanity's extraordinary potential. The compassion, love and understanding built into women's hearts complements the aggressive warrior male spirit, and this union beautifully displays the splendor and complexity of God's nature. For us to experience the revival for which we pray, the fullness of His character must be revealed in the unity of the family of God—men and women, mothers and fathers, sisters and brothers—demonstrating His goodness and revealing His love. This may not come easily, but if we rely on the Holy Spirit and make space for one another to become all that God has called us to be, we will find grace for the journey. Lord, let it be so to your glory.

Partial Bibliography

Bristow, John, What Paul Really Said About Women, Harper Collins, San Francisco, CA, 1988

Edwards, Gene, The Christian Woman...Set Free, Seedsowers, Jacksonville, FL, 2005

Grady, J. Lee, 10 Lies the Church Tells Women, Charisma House, Lake Mary, FL, 2000

Grady, J. Lee, 25 Tough Questions About Women and the Church, Charisma House, Lake Mary, FL, 2003

Johnson, Alan, How I Changed My Mind About Women in Leadership, Zondervan, Grand Rapids, MI, 2010

King, Susan, Who Is the Helper, http://cwgministries.org/who-is-the-helper, accessed March 2017

Mowcxko, Margaret, Various Articles on Women in Leadership, http://newlife.id.au/ accessed March 2017

Perriman, A. C., What Eve Did, What Women Shouldn't Do, http://www.tyndalehouse.com/tynbul/library/TynBull_1993_44_1_08_Perriman_EvelTim2.pdf, accessed March 2017

Silk, Danny, Powerful and Free, Red Arrow Media, Redding, CA, 2012